W9-CNY-789

BEYOND THE COLD WAR

A NEW APPROACH TO THE ARMS RACE AND NUCLEAR ANNIHILATION

ALSO BY E. P. THOMPSON

The Making of the English Working Class

Whigs and Hunters

William Morris: Romantic to Revolutionary

Albion's Fatal Tree

BEYOND THE COLD WAR

A NEW APPROACH TO THE ARMS RACE AND NUCLEAR ANNIHILATION

E.P. THOMPSON

PANTHEON BOOKS, NEW YORK

 Published in the United States by Pantheon Books, a division of Random House, Inc., New York, and simultaneously in Canada by Random House of Canada Limited, Toronto. Originally published in United Kingdom as *Zero Option* by The Merlin Press.

Library of Congress Cataloging in Publication Data

Thompson, E. P. (Edward Palmer), 1924–
Beyond the cold war.

1. Atomic weapons and disarmament. I. Title.
JX1974.7.T525 1982 327.1'74 82-47896
ISBN 0-394-52796-8
ISBN 0-394-71218-8 (pbk.)

Since all acknowledgements cannot be accommodated on the copyright page, they are to be found on pages 197–198.

Manufactured in the United States of America
First American Edition

CONTENTS

To
W.H. and Carol Ferry

A PREFACE IN SACKCLOTH

I am sitting at my desk, in Worcester, England, on June 9, 1982, trying to write a message to American readers. It is an impossible task. For two months British political life has been dominated by one thing: the war in the Falkland Islands. Four days ago another war commenced, and Israeli forces are now on the outskirts of Beirut. Today British forces are poised for a final assault on Port Stanley, and another British frigate has been damaged (perhaps sunk) by the Argentine air force. Yesterday Pantheon's courteous editor got onto me on the transatlantic line—could I send my preface for the American edition? It must be today or never.

Yes, I do wish to send a message to friends in the United States. But whatever I write will be overtaken by events by the time my copy gets to Pantheon's offices: by the time it is published it will be long overtaken.

What I really wish to do, now, is to come before the American public in a mood of unaccustomed penitence. Some of the articles and essays in this book were written a year or more ago, when the British and European peace movements were getting going but when American opinion was still sluggish and (for a long while) dazed by the Iranian hostages episode. I wrote a version of my essay 'Protest and Survive', which was generously presented in the United States (by *The Nation* and by Monthly Review Press) in the form of 'A Letter to Americans'. Maybe I seemed to be a little truculent in this; maybe some readers found my tone to be scolding, as I contrasted the new developments in European opinion with the United States during the 'yellow ribbon' hysteria and at the time of President Reagan's election.

Yes, I did find American military strategies and gargantuan arms budgeting to be scarey, and the militarist and bullying mood of some politicians and much of the media to be ugly. So did very many of my American friends. I don't retract the judgements which I made then — for example my description (in 'A Show for the European Theatre') of a mood of 'isolationism armed with nukes'.

But Britain, as I write, has withdrawn into its own mood of isolationism, armed with a task-force, and our own politicians and much of our media have been quite as bullying and ugly. Opponents of the Falklands War have been accused of 'treachery' or have been denounced as 'left fascists', in language which reminded me of the worst bits of the Hearst and Scripps-Howard press in the United States in 1946 — the prelude to full McCarthyism. It has been a replay, in some ways, of the Iranian hostages crisis in the United States. The Falkland Islanders have been the hostages, and the dominating issue has been injured national self-esteem. In a sense, the British task-force has been Mrs Thatcher's helicopter rescue operation — yet one which was not providentially aborted before its very dangerous consequences began to be disclosed.

No Briton today has any business to rant and scold about peace to anyone. Maybe I ought to come before you in sackcloth and ashes. A loud part of our popular media — incited by our government — has become very ugly, pandering to sensationalism and vicarious violence, and shot through with imperialist nostalgia and deliberately-contrived World War II reminiscence. And a part of the British public have been sitting nightly around their TV sets, excited out of their minds by a real-life open-ended serial in the South Atlantic.

I say 'a part of the British public'. No, not all of us. A sober portion of the public has watched this whole episode with anxiety and has learned from it quite different lessons. It is not that the whole peace movement, or CND (the Campaign for Nuclear Disarmament), repudiated the sending of a task-force out of pacifist principle: only a minority of the peace movement are absolute pacifists. Many members of the movement felt that — whatever the merits of the Argentinian claim — the Argentine aggression ought to be repudiated, and that the Falkland Islanders' rights ought to be defended against a singularly unpleasant fascist militarism. Most of us held that this should be done by economic and diplomatic measures, with the support of the United Nations (in pursuance of Resolution 502). But others were willing, in the early stages —

and perhaps up until the sinking of the *General Belgrano* — to go along with the sending out of a British task-force, which they assumed was a piece of bluff, and part of the repertoire of diplomacy.

Among the many lessons learned are these: first, we have observed an object-lesson in the logic of military escalation. Step by step the stakes have been raised: force on one side has called forth a response of force on the other: national pride has called forth the national pride of the Other. Once set in motion, the military necessities of the task-force have taken over from the intentions of the politicians who sent the task-force out. It is exactly such a sequence of mutually-enforcing two-sided escalation which could lead us into the last nuclear war.

It is sometimes asked: would any statesmen in their right minds permit a nuclear exchange? We know the answer now. When a course of military confrontation is embarked upon, statemanship gives way before military exigencies, and after a few days none of the operators are in their right minds any more.

Second, we have learned — as we have learned from earlier episodes, and as we are learning once more from Israel's invasion of the Lebanon — of the disastrous inadequacy of the United Nations, the immense fragility of any attempt to establish an international rule of law. The peace movement has to take this into the heart of its concerns, throughout the world.

Third, we have learned once more how slender are the cultural and political defences against the surge of nationalism, when both politicians and the popular media license this atavism.

Fourth, the Falklands War has brought home to us the intimate relations between militarism at home — and as expressed in the confrontation between NATO and the Warsaw blocs — and the export of militarism (as well as advanced weaponry) to the proliferating military juntas of the Third World.

None of these lessons can leave Britons feeling loud and self-righteous. After all (lesson four) it was President Carter, in the name of human rights, who cut off arms supplies to Argentina, and it was Britain, France and Israel that cut themselves in on the trade. Which led us, in the British peace movement, sharply to a fifth lesson. The militarisms of other nations (including the United States) may be pretty awful. But our first job is to control our own. You must allow us a little space for honourable national feeling. If

Mrs Thatcher is to be brought down, we would like to take some part in doing this ourselves.

It was generally put around, in this country and abroad, that the British peace movement was finished, knocked sideways by the Falklands War. There had been arranged, very long ago, a national demonstration in Hyde Park in London on June 6 to signal the opening of the United Nations Second Special Session on Disarmament. It was said on all sides that the event would be a flop, and a deadly blow to CND's morale. Even some organisers and speakers were biting their nails. Then the day came — three days ago as I am writing — and the peace movement moved in to the park, with scarcely a dent in its numbers. On October 24 last year we were some quarter of a million strong: on June 6, at the height of the Falklands War and of media abuse, maybe 200,000 or 220,000. The banners came from every corner of the British Isles: the 'other Britain' assembled to affirm its presence in our national life. And, in solidarity, the speakers and contingents from other national movements came in even greater strength than before, to bring us reassurance in a moment of difficulty.

That was (as I am now writing) three days ago. And in three day's time the UN Special Assembly will be signalled by a great demonstration in New York. The size of that event will already be history by the time that you read these lines. All I will say is this: the peace movement in Britain has been through a rough two months and it may get even rougher just ahead. We are here still, and there is nothing that will make us go away.

But this really is a good moment for the United States cavalry to come pouring over the hill — or, at least, for the tens and hundreds of thousands of American peace-workers who have filled the Rose Bowl, LA, Central Park, Manhattan, and dozens of other places across the United States. This will give us, in Europe, the strength and morale for a second blow.

9 June 1982 E.P.Thompson

INTRODUCTION

The 'zero option' which this book advocates is a nuclear-free Europe. A nuclear-free world would, of course, be better. We can opt for that also. But we can work, effectively, only for what is within our reach. There is a powerful movement also for a nuclear-free Pacific, which brings together Japan, Australia, and the Pacific islanders who continue to be threatened by nuclear weapons' tests. There is another, less powerful, movement to clear nuclear weapons from the Indian Ocean.

These movements are our natural allies. There is nothing privileged about Europe nor about European life. For three decades war has been most common in the Third World, and on occasion (Korea, Vietnam, Afghanistan) the advanced nations have exported their violence: what has been a Cold War here has been a good deal hotter there.

Why, then, a movement specific to this continent, for European nuclear disarmament? This is not just one more example of our Eurocentric vision. It is, first, because there are particular military and strategic dispositions on this continent which present a particular threat and which, at the same time, dictate the need for common action by Europeans in defence of peace. And it is, second, because there are political and cultural conditions unique to Europe which present us with particular responsibilities and opportunities.

The political and military conditions peculiar to Europe, although long present, became fully visible with the decision of NATO of December 12th, 1979, to 'modernise' its continental nuclear weaponry. From this decision may be dated, also, the genesis of the movement for European nuclear disarmament. For the decision made visible, in the same moment, the definition of Europe, in the contingency plans of the Pentagon, as a possible 'theatre' of limited nuclear war. The decision impelled into existence a movement of opposition within the five recipient nations (Holland, Belgium, Britain, West Germany and Italy) and their Scandinavian neighbours.

This movement may, in its first appearance, have been reflexive and self-regarding. For what became suddenly visible–not to defence 'experts' only but to the general public–was the density of nuclear weapons and of bases (and hence also of targets) on this continent: densest of all in Central Europe, and next in the British Isles. Yet this is not all that the European peace movement has been about: 'no cruise, no Pershing II, no SS-20s!' For as anxiety and discourse among the national movements have grown, so also people have been led to question the political conditions which divide Europe into two parts and which engender, in the adversary blocs, this growth in weaponry. And the internationalism of protest which first grew up in the West has begun to seek (and sometimes to find) routes through to like-minded groups in the East.

At the simplest level, the European peace movements have expressed a rising consciousness of domination by the two great superpowers, and of the reduction of lesser nations (whether in NATO or the Warsaw Pact) to client status in their military and diplomatic roles. That small elite of persons which is sometimes known (absurdly) as 'the defence community' regards such questions as closed. The ineluctable condition of bloc antagonism is taken, unexamined, as a premise from which all else flows. Once within such premises it is never possible to get out–and the same premises are shared by 'the defence community' of both sides. With every exit blocked off by worst-case hypotheses as to the strategies and weapons of the other side, there is nowhere else to go except into arguments about weapons 'balance' or exercises in 'arms control'. The experts ask us to leave it to them (perhaps behind closed doors at Geneva), since any 'political' intrusion will afford an entry to forces or emotions extraneous to their equilibrium: and this might induce 'instability'.

Politics is thus walled out by the first premise of deterrence theory–that the two blocs are in a state of perpetual armed hostility and must ever continue to be so. Hence any attempt at political resolution is postponed, and weapons serve as a substitute.

Yet as the peace movement has contested particular weapons, so the premises of deterrence have begun to crumble, and, in the same moment, new political options have been disclosed. As we examine the seemingly value-free assumptions and strategies of the 'experts' they turn out not to be founded upon any secure military rationale (although they are subsequently rationalised in this way) but to arise from ulterior political considerations. The number of SS-20s in deployment by the Soviet Union is not a question of military 'security' but one of political bargaining and 'face'. There never was (it is now widely admitted even within 'the defence community') a sound military case for the deployment of cruise and Pershing II, but we are stuck with the beastly things because we must show to the Soviet Union the united political resolve of NATO.

What is needed is less 'arms control' than control of the political and military leaders who deploy these arms. And it is *this* which is (in the eyes of those leaders) the peace movement's great offence. 'Oh, those demonstrations', said President Reagan in December 1981: 'Those are all sponsored by a thing called the World Peace Council, which is bought and paid for by the Soviet Union.' He knows this to be a lie: but he would *like* it to be true. Everything would then be simple and in its proper place. But Mr Brezhnev would like it to be true also. For the peace movement is equally incomprehensible to those ageing Soviet leaders who find that they *cannot* manipulate it, that it will not fall within the strategies of the World Peace Council, that it makes demands also on them and supports *both* the cause of peace and that of civil rights.

The peace movement founded itself upon the simplest of premises: the defence of civilisation, the defence of the ecosphere—the human ecological imperative. Yet this simple premise removed it, at a bound, from the premises of the 'defence community' of both sides: those of 'balance' in 'deterrence'. And, in the same moment, a whole new field of political possibilities was revealed, which had remained hidden and constrained within the premises of the Cold War.

This movement is a new phenomenon, which scarcely yet knows itself or can articulate its own demands. In 1980 and in 1981 it was strongest in Europe, a continent broken by the Cold War into two artificial halves. In these particular political conditions it was inevitable that Europeans should begin to search once more for a third way between the opposed superpowers. This search is taking many forms. Individuals, churches, professional groups (like the physicians) have taken their own initiatives. Nuclear-free zones have been declared by elected authorities, and these are commencing exchanges with each other. The question of larger nuclear-free zones (Nordic, Balkan, Central European) has entered the political agenda of states. Petitioners in both Germanies have raised the question of the long-protracted presence of NATO and of Warsaw Pact forces upon German soil—and of the threat which this perpetual state of confrontation presents in the heart of Europe—and have proposed the need for peace treaties and for the withdrawal not only of nuclear weapons but of conventional troops. A dialogue has been opened between Western peace movements and persons working for civil and trade union rights in the Warsaw Pact states. It becomes more and more evident that the question of weapons and the question of the greater autonomy of states to effect their own diplomatic initiatives—that is, the gradual break-up of both blocs—must be taken together.

It is this new field of political possibility which defines the character of a peace movement specific to Europe. Europeans have particular opportunities to commence, by trial and error, to break down the ideological and security structures of the Cold War in their own midst. This is not a matter of European privilege but of European responsibilities towards the rest of the world. It is not fear only but also the excitement of these newly-disclosed opportunities which is seizing the imagination of a younger generation of Europeans.

The 'defence' establishments of both sides are alarmed by the spontaneity and lack of deference of the movement: they see it as 'de-stabilising'. They seek to constrain it within traditional political forms and categories, and to confine all the turbulent waters of popular demonstrations into a stagnant lake of secretive negotiations about 'balance', conducted with due propriety by the proper and authorised personnel of the rival establishments. If this was to happen then the chance of a third way to peace would be lost. That is why the peace movement must continue to influence the political process, but from outside its forms and independent of its controls. It must remain autonomous and non-aligned.

This book includes most of my interventions, in writing, for the peace movement from 1980 until early 1982, except for *Protest and Survive.* Like many others I served my apprenticeship in the early days of CND (and before that in opposition to the Korean War); but my involvement in the new movement dates from the run-up to the NATO modernisation decision of 12th December 1979. A group of us, working closely with CND, formed a committee for European Nuclear Disarmament; and we issued an Appeal, in April 1980, for a nuclear-free Europe, sometimes known as the 'Russell Appeal' because of the major role played by the Bertrand Russell Peace Foundation in circulating it for signature throughout Western Europe.

At about the same time I wrote *Protest and Survive* (at first as a pamphlet)–and since that time I have been without cease on the stump for END. The mail flowing into our house, not only from Britain but from Europe, North America, Australia, has been overwhelming; and, welcome as it has been, it has also been painful to have to refuse so many warm invitations to speak and to turn away correspondents with such inadequate replies. END has developed its own professional office–in constant communication with like-minded movements in Europe and across the Atlantic–CND has grown by leaps and bounds into a major national force, and friendly associated movements (the Friends, long-standing peace groups, the World Disarmament Campaign) have all contributed to the regenerated movement.

I mention these details because nothing is more absurd than the notion of the peace movement as some kind of conspiracy, or as a disciplined phalanx, 'orchestrated' (as Caspar Weinberger supposes) by Moscow. I have never known in my own lifetime any movement whose growth has been more spontaneous, untidy, and unplanned–and I have studied, as a social historian, few movements with comparable spontaneity. The movement has always grown at a pace much faster than its offices or resources could keep up with. A few of us who happened to come forward, as writers, organisers or speakers, in those early days of 1980 have been thrown into prominence by the massive arousal all around us–have been adopted by the media as Personalities and spokespersons–and have become the prisoners of a movement which we heartily welcome but did not, in our most sanguine moments, expect.

We are willing prisoners. But it would be presumptuous and mistaken to regard ourselves as 'leaders'. We may offer, each of us, our own analysis and proposals, as I do in several of the essays which follow. But if I am correct that the European peace movements signal entry upon a quite new field of political possibility in our continent, then what is paramount is that this field remains *open*: the dialogue, the exchanges, the search for third ways, the hesitant discourse between East and West by a hundred unofficial routes–these are still, at this stage, what are most important. There must be a wide tolerance of disagreements within the European peace movement. It does not require competing authoritative leaders nor yet a governing central committee.

It is very certainly an untidy movement. In some nations its organisation is so inchoate that it is more a political mood than a movement. Or it is a mood made manifest, as in the great demonstrations in Europe's capital cities in October and November 1981, when socialists, ecologists, Christians of many denominations, liberals, Eurocommunists, feminists, trade unionists, and, above all, young people of varied persuasions made their presence felt and broke through the barricades of the servile official media.

I am not exalting the virtues of untidiness. I am only emphasising the movement's spontaneity. This peace movement has been bought and paid for by no-one. It has been bought and paid for by itself, and it is jealous of its independence. Very certainly, greater co-ordination and more professional communications are necessary: and this is what much of the work of our own END Committee has been about. But this–the work of publications, delegations, conferences and conventions, or of the Vienna Peace Festival–is the work of communication, not of control.

Of course, however new the field of possibilities, strategies must be worked out and choices must be made. There are disagreements within national movements, and there are in several countries World Peace Council interventions which seek to divert support into simplistic pro-Soviet courses. I am not against open arguments, and my own 'Disarmament and Human Rights' and 'Beyond the Cold War' are arguments of this sort, which take up positions on questions of peace and civil rights sharper than some of my colleagues would share. What I am against is any premature closure or narrowing of the debate. Communication must precede the coming to conclusions, and the work of communication has only half commenced.

We already have, within the European peace movements and on their margins, an extraordinary and rich discourse. Even in terms of associated political groups, the confluence is remarkable: the Greens in West Germany and Plaid Cymru in Wales, Eurocommunists in South Europe and Social Democrats in the North, PASOK in Greece and the Progressive Party in Iceland, in Ireland a nuclear-free Cork and also a nuclear-free Belfast. And when we move out of the formal political groupings into the less formal affinities of youth and women's movements, scholars and writers, the popular music world, then the confluence is even wider. The banners come in every colour–although rarely, as yet, in blue–and all are drawn together in the common rainbow of resistance to nuclear war.

Yet this work of communication has only half commenced, not only because we have scarcely learned to understand each other, but also because there are still new constituencies to gather in. The movement has advanced unevenly, now swiftly, now seeming to be stationary or even in withdrawal, like water breaking in upon uneven land. Commencing in Holland, Belgium, Norway, it broke into Britain by the late Spring of 1980 and spread steadily thereafter. But there was little sign of any movement of mass dimension in West

Germany until the Protestant church-day in Hamburg in June 1981. It gathered way then with astonishing rapidity, and by September an even more rapid growth in the popular movement could be seen in Italy. By the time of the autumn demonstrations the movement seemed to be everywhere—Helsinki, Berne, Athens, Madrid. . . And now, as I write (in April 1982), the latest arrival—so swift that it has unbalanced President Reagan—has been the powerful movement for a nuclear freeze in the United States.

And yet it is not quite 'everywhere' as yet. In Western Europe one great nation, France, has remained a quiet constituency—not altogether quiet, of course, yet standing a little apart. Yet how can we put Europe back together if France is not an active party? And, above all, communication between West and East Europe—direct, unrestricted communication between persons and movements—remains gummed up by ideologists and bureaucrats, or confused by false appearances and misrecognitions. A start has been made: there are elements of an independent, non-aligned peace movement in East Germany and in Hungary: voices reach us from Czechoslovakia, Poland and the Soviet Union: and in Roumania there have been demonstrations in support of a nuclear-free Europe, with slogans critical of the weaponry of both superpowers. Yet this is only a start. It gives to us a bare possibility of survival. If possibility is to become probability, then our communications must break through, to a hundred unofficial constituencies, in the East.

Even well-intentioned statesmen and orators before the United Nations tend to get matters in the wrong order. They wish to work out some neat arrangements for peace-keeping or arms control between the great states first of all, and they suppose that internationalism will follow on. What follow, in fact, are windy declarations, more and more arms, and public cynicism or international ill-will. The peace movement, in 1980–2, has got the order right. It has been building a foundation of internationalism, in its publications, conferences and demonstrations. If the statesmen now can work out some neat arrangements for disarmament, we have prepared the ground that these can stand upon.

The spontaneous generation of an internationalism of

resistance to every form of militarisation is the necessary task of this living generation, in these immediate years. It is the greatest gift we can give to the future; and if we do not do it well then there will not be a future. And everyone can take a hand in doing this. This is an internationalism which does not wait upon the permission of authorities, or run only along bureaucratic channels. It can be done by publications and by musicians, by attending each others' demonstrations, by formal conferences and, informally, in a wine-shop or a coffee-bar on vacations, by correspondence and by exchanges in the professions, by twinning nuclear-free zones and by twinning movements. The only internationalism worth anything must be founded upon the experience and exchanges of multitudes.

And this can also be good fun. Some of the work as a prisoner of the movement can be taxing and wearisome, as we confront, with our pitifully inadequate resources, the tax-supported establishments of the armed states. But I have had more than my fair share of the work's rewards. I have been supported, not only by the well-informed and determined movement to be found in every part of Britain, but I have also had the good fortune to get about a good deal in Europe and in the United States. Everywhere I have met with the same determination, the same optimism of the will, the same sense of opening possibility: in Oslo, Helsinki, North Carolina, West Berlin, Dublin, Copenhagen, Los Angeles.

I will select two examples, fresh in my memory, on the stomp in Ireland and in Iceland in March 1982. I had been warned in England not to expect too much of the Irish movement, least of all in the North which was too preoccupied with its own troubles to take in the problems of the world. The warning proved to be long out-of-date. I would like to describe the inspiring meetings at Liberty Hall in Dublin, at Maynooth College, in Galway and in Belfast: the discussions about Irish neutrality and how this might be put effectively to use alongside the non-aligned powers: the concern that Ireland might be bribed or bullied into NATO, or that the North might provide bases for sea- and air-launched cruise missiles if the European peace movement should succeed in expelling their quota from the ground.

Here were questions which united Irish persons of whatever faith, and which impelled them into the international community of resistance. And I remember a packed meeting in Derry, the audience in the main young men and women from the Catholic neighbourhood. It was a good meeting, not because of my performance but in spite of it: I had a headache, was uncertain of the interests of the audience, and laboured too many abstract arguments. The questions were serious, well-informed and outward-looking. These young citizens of Derry—many of them unemployed and with no prospect of employment, living in a tense, divided and inward-turning city—had found in the peace movement a way to break out of their isolation and to reclaim their place in internationalism. In resistance to militarism they had discovered a new kind of hope. The next day the small office of the Derry Anti Nuclear Group, staffed by an unpaid unemployed worker, went up in flames as an incendiary device went off in a paint-shop below. Rumour had it that no particular ill-will was held by anyone to DANG: the device was planted there by error. No matter: the intellectual capital of months of work—the membership records, the files of cuttings and of information, the correspondence—were burned in a few minutes, and the staff were lucky not to go with them. At the Belfast meeting that night, when the news was given, a bucket went around for contributions to set DANG on its feet again. And on its feet again it is. For less than two weeks afterwards it had opened up a new office, next door to the one that was burned. That is a movement which has settled in, deep into a community, and which means to stay.

In Iceland there need be no doubt about the movement's staying-power, since it is older than most of the new generation of European peace movements. There has been a movement against NATO bases ever since NATO bullied Iceland into granting these during the Korean War. The present Campaign against Military Bases was founded, from the merging of existing movements, in 1972. For much of this time Icelanders have campaigned alone, or with little support from Europe.

What has given a new urgency to the Icelandic campaign is, ironically, the very success of the European movements. For if cruise and Pershing II are refused on European territory, then it is probable that more and more missiles will be put to sea. The supposed 'gate' in the North Atlantic, between Norway (and North Scotland) on one hand, and Iceland on the other, is now a highly sensitive strategic area. Here nuclear-armed submarines already patrol, and through this 'gate' (NATO strategists surmise) Soviet Backfire bombers could come down, from the Kola peninsula, through Europe's back-door.

Hence the generals in their war-games rooms busy themselves with scenarios which emphasise Iceland's enhanced strategic significance. And hence also the Icelandic Campaign sees clearly the links between their own NATO base at Keflavik and the development of NATO's base in Stornoway in the Western Isles. It sees also the need to draw closer its ties with European movements, with the Scottish Campaign against Trident, with British and Irish CND, with the Norwegian 'No to Nuclear Weapons', and with the campaign for a Nordic Nuclear-Free Zone.

On March 27th, 1982, my wife and I were guests of the Icelandic Campaign at a meeting in Reykjavik. The population of Iceland is some 240,000 of whom one-third live in the Icelandic capital. One thousand two hundred people filled to overflowing the largest meeting-place in Iceland, a cinema. It was a moving and highly-professional meeting, with speeches, musicians, and with young actors and actresses reciting poems and sketches. A leading young dramatist conducted the proceedings. Our message of European solidarity met with the most generous response. I convey their message of solidarity with our own movement, in return, to the reader.

Icelanders have one of the most enduring, most tenacious, material and spiritual cultures on this earth. Theirs is an inhospitable environment, with a brief summer, scanty resources, and a severe climate. For more than one thousand years they have wrested a livelihood from the sea and the grass, passing on their literature, their laws and their faith. Icelandic culture would never have survived through that millenium if each living generation had not held stubbornly to its duty as trustee, holding in its care the passage between a hard past and an uncertain future.

In this the Icelanders seemed to symbolise what our peace movement is about. We also have such duties as trustees. And this remarkable meeting in Reykjavik gave one a sudden flicker of hope—that it is still possible that we might succeed. One imagined the generals in their war-games room pouring over the map of the North Atlantic 'gate'—Greenland there, the Faeroes there, Stornoway there, the Kola peninsula up there. And then, here, in the midst of it all, this wonderful military asset, this great block of land with its ice-caps and fjords and lava-beds—a splendid place for bases, for air-strips and AWACS and for submarine installations. Iceland! No problem there: the perfect pivot for the total militarisation of the North Atlantic ocean.

And yet, in their calculations, the generals had overlooked one thing: the enduring passion for independence of the Icelanders, the tenacity of the human spirit. That summoning of spirit, that trusteeship, and that internationalism is what our peace movement is about.

DETERRENCE AND ADDICTION

I will not take up the time of this conference expounding my own views as to the immorality, or even the insanity, of the weaponry which is legitimated by the theory of deterrence. My views on this are sufficiently known. Similar views have been expressed by many others. Mr George F. Kennan, in an article in the *New York Review of Books* (July 16, 1981), has written:

> To my mind, the nuclear bomb is the most useless weapon ever invented. It can be employed to no constructive purpose. It is not even an effective defense against itself.

Immoral or insane, the weapons are now here, in superabundance. They condition our behaviour and our expectations in innumerable ways. The consequences of their use defy our imagination. But, at the same time, the dismantling of all this weaponry, down to the last nuclear land-mine, by the mutual agreement of both blocs and of other proliferating parties, would require such a total redirection of strategy, resources, ideologies, diplomacies—such an unprecedented investment in agitation, negotiation, and conversion—that this exhausts our imagination also. In confronting the threat to civilisation we are, in the end, confronting ourselves; we turn away from the mirror, exhausted and self-defeated. We will pass the problem on, unresolved, to the next generation or the generation that follows. If any generation does.

This is, essentially, the political meaning of contemporary deterrence theory. In its pure form, that of MAD, or Mutual Assured Destruction, it proposes that war between the super-

---

Paper delivered to the British Association for the Advancement of Science (General Section), York, September 1981.

powers and their allies may be indefinitely postponed because nuclear weapons make any alternative unthinkable or unacceptable. I emphasise 'postponement'. The theory does not propose the victory of one 'side' over the other 'side', neither does it propose the resolution of those differences between the two parties which might, purportedly, bring them to war. On the contrary, by maintaining each party in a posture of menace to the other, it fixes indefinitely the tension which makes the resolution of differences improbable. It transfixes diplomacies and ideologies into a twilight state; while postponing war it postpones also the resolution of peace.

This would be so even if we were to succeed in reducing weaponry to a level of minimal deterrence: let us say six delivery-systems on each side. (In fact, as I will argue later, one major constituent of the meaning of nuclear weapons is *symbolic;* and a reduction to this level would signal so great a symbolic victory for rationality that the threat of the remaining weapons would be increasingly fictitious and the space for political resolutions would enlarge.) But we are not reducing weaponry. Over the past two decades this has been steadily increasing, not only in gross destructive power–as Mr Kennan has said, 'levels of redundancy of such grotesque dimensions as to defy rational understanding'–but also in the quality and accuracy of delivery-systems. Hence the theory of deterrence now legitimates, not Mutual Assured Destruction, but Mutual Aggravated Destruction. And to the degree that menace is aggravated with each year, the resolution of differences by means short of war becomes less probable. There is no longer an even-handed postponement both of war and of peace; terminal war becomes more likely, the terminus of peace recedes from any agenda.

Is such a consequence inherent in the premises of the theory itself? On the one hand, it can be argued that this need not necessarily be so. A rigidly-enforced state of minimal deterrence, policed by some international authority, need not be subject to the law of aggravation. On the other hand, it has been argued, persuasively, that deterrence is inherently addictive, and hence must lead to aggravation. In 1979, shortly before his death, Professor Gregory Bateson, a member of the Board of Regents of the University of

California, addressed his fellow Regents with the plea that the University renounce any part in the research or development of nuclear weapons. Employing analogies from biological systems as transferred to social psychology, he argued that

> the short-time deterrent effect is achieved at the expense of long-time cumulative change. The actions which today postpone disaster result in an increase in strength on *both* sides of the competitive system to ensure a greater instability and greater destruction if and when the explosion occurs. It is this fact of cumulative change from one act of threat to the next that gives the system the quality of *addiction.*

Bateson reminds us that we are not just dealing with weapons, in a medium of pure theory, where one threat balances and cancels out the other. These weapons operate in the medium of politics, ideology and strategy; they are perceived as menacing and are intended to be so; they induce fear and they simultaneously enhance and frustrate feelings of aggression. Nor need aggravation pursue a steady linear advancement: in the vocabulary of mathematical catastrophe theory civilisation may already be tipping over upon the overhanging cusp between fear and aggression.

This is really enough, and more than enough, about deterrence as theory. It is in truth a pitiful, light-weight theory. It is espoused, in its pristine purity, only by a handful of monkish celibates, retired within the walls of centres of Strategic Studies. It cannot endure any intercourse with the actual world. It is at heart a very simple, and simple-minded, idea, which occurred to the first cave men when they got hold of clubs. (It is this very simplicity which gives to it a certain populist plausibility.) If I have a club, that will deter him from clobbering me. The thought has gone on, through armies and empires, dreadnoughts and gas; all that a historian can say is that sometimes it has worked for a while, and sometimes it has not, but always in the end it has broken down. All that is new about it now is that the clubs of today, the technology of destruction, are so immense as to defy any rational exercise. It is this which made an old (and massively-disproved) theory appear plausible once more, for a while. It seemed, for a time, that the new weapons were so terrible that they could be employed, not to fight, but to *avert* war.

But it is not an *operative* theory: that is, it does not direct any nation's behaviour. It appears always as a gloss, as an *ex post facto* apologia, as a theoretical legitimation of actions which are taken for quite different reasons. The first atomic weapons were not developed because some theorist invented deterrence, and *then* scientists were commissioned to invent a bomb. The bombs were invented to blast the German and Japanese antagonists into submission. US Strategic Air Command was then established, in 1946, not to deter Soviet nuclear attack, but to threaten a United States first strike against Russia. Thermo-nuclear weapons were not developed to deter anyone, but to demonstrate United States military superiority, and because it seemed to be a sweet new device worth developing. It was only *after* the Soviet Union also developed thermo-nuclear weapons that the theory of deterrence came into vogue, and on both sides. But if the theory had been operative, instead of cosmetic, that is where the development of such weaponry would have come to a fixed point of rest. Of course it did not. Development—aggravated menace—has gone on and on. It has been led, in almost every case, by the United States, and the Soviet Union has never passed up an opportunity to answer or match each development. Maybe (but I find the whole argument about 'balance', when we are in these regions of grotesque overkill, to be absurd) in this or that particular of delivery-systems the Soviet Union is now ahead.

This was not done by a theory. If the theory, in its pure form, has ever had any operative force, it has perhaps been on the Russian side, at the time when they were developing their first mega-rockets capable of delivering weapons onto United States territory. Khrushchev is the nearest we can get to a philosopher king of deterrence. But since his time the theory has long been admixed with more powerful, and operative, interests and inertias. If Soviet military theory today dispenses with repeated incantations about 'deterrence', this may be because Soviet strategists have less need to bear in mind the cosmetic, public-relations functions of theory.

There is now a substantial literature on the weapons-system complex as an effective *interest*. I do not mean to rehearse it. There has never been a stationary state of mutual deterrence; instead there has been a ceaseless pursuit for advantage *within* that state. The operative pressures have come both from the regions of politics and ideology, and from the inertial thrust of research and development—sometimes known as 'technology creep'—within the military-industrial complexes of the opposed powers. Deterrence theory did not give us Poseidon and Polaris, the SS-20, the cruise missiles, the neutron bomb. These were given to us by the 'alchemists' in the research laboratories, the arms lobbyists, the alarmist leader-writers and populist politicians, and by the inter-service competition of the military elites. Deterrence theory came in afterwards, to excuse all these things.

In doing so it has become ever less credible, and more spattered with the impurities of the real actors. The Awful yet Sublime doctrine of MAD has given way to sub-doctrines which clearly pursue strategic or tactical advantage; which spell out scenarios in which nuclear wars become thinkable once again—first and second strike capability, counterforce, flexible response, notions of 'limited' nuclear war. Each one of these theories demands more, and more accurate, and more technically-sweet, weapons in order to 'deter' not what does exist but what might, in theory, exist on the other side in future. In most cases these weapons are already under development, and are in search of a theory to excuse them. And in all cases they actually hasten on the response of the other side—that is the answering weapons which they were, supposedly, to deter.

We know, as a well-established point of method, that it is more possible to *dis*prove a theory than to prove it. But few of us would wish to see the theory of deterrence disproved, in a definitive manner, for the satisfaction (if we remained alive) of having won an argument. There are, however, other ways of demonstrating that a theory is suspect. One may examine its intellectual credentials, enquire what kind of a theory it is, and to which discipline it belongs.

When a theory can be employed (as this theory is) to endorse *every* new development in strategy and in weaponry

–when one knows, in advance, that this will be done–then one has every reason to suppose that one is dealing with ideology, with the apologetics of power. This may appear as unfair to certain distinguished practitioners, who employ the theory with subtlety and who effect distinctions between strategies and between weapons. But what impresses here is the subtlety of the practitioner, not of the theory; there is no fire-break of any *theoretical* kind between the concepts employed in the scholarly strategic journals and the same concepts vulgarised in *Hansard* or in the popular press.

Deterrence theory in fact covers an immense intellectual spectrum. In its most debased, populist form it is sheer humbug. It has even spawned itself as a noun, descriptive of *our* thermo-nuclear weaponry (but rarely of theirs): 'the deterrent'. There cannot be *a* deterrent. It may be possible to justify the deployment of a weapon capable of effecting the extermination of multitudes within *a theory* of deterrence. But to speak of '*a* deterrent' is to ascribe the intentions (or purported intentions) of the users to the weapon itself, as part of its inherent quality. Yet that weapon will remain the same weapon, even if the intentions of the users change: or if terrorists were to capture it and carry it off for other uses. Those who refer to 'our deterrent' or 'the British deterrent' are guilty of the pathetic fallacy, which, while pardonable in the lines of poets, is something worse than pathetic in the mouths of politicians and military experts. For this usage pre-empts enquiry by attributing normative qualities–and highly desirable normative qualities at that–to this thing in the very same instant as the thing itself is indicated. 'Deterrence' (ideology on every side insists) is a good strategy; our statesmen must be good guys whose intentions cannot be questioned–even if our side does happen to reserve to itself the right of first nuclear strike; therefore the strategy and the good intentions can slither off onto the weaponry itself. If we are reassured in every moment of usage, in the prescribed vocabulary of public discourse, that weapons are only 'deterrents', then the more we have of them the better.

I am sorry to labour the point. I am sorry that it is necessary to do so. But these little points of vocabulary and usage add to the inertial thrust which is carrying us towards the Final Solution. Any politician who refers to '*the* deterrent' is either so slapdash in his logic that he merits our suspicion, or he is dealing knowingly in humbug.

At the other end of the intellectual spectrum—but employing the same family of concepts—are the specialist, prestigious, and well-funded academic think-tanks and periodicals. Not all that has gone on in these has always been rubbish. Serious empirical work has been done, especially in the heyday of the arms control community in the United States during the negotiation of the two SALT treaties. The more recent lurch into ideology has been signalled by the withdrawal of many reputable scholars of an older generation. For it is from an older generation of strategists, arms controllers and scientific advisers, and diplomats—among them Kennan, York, Scoville, Warnke, La Rocque, and Lords Mountbatten and Zuckerman—that some of the most sombre warnings as to our present predicament have come.

My own first acquaintance with the vocabulary of deterrence theory is relatively recent. I was unfamiliar with its terms and permutations when my eye alighted, in astonishment, upon a letter from Professor Michael Howard in the correspondence columns of *The Times* (January 30, 1980). I promptly poured out the vials of my polemic upon Professor Howard's head, unaware that my wrath should have been directed at the general theory of deterrence, with its curiously-hermetic vocabulary, limited to posture and worst-case expectations—a vocabulary not invented by Professor Howard, and which consorts uneasily with his richer historical and military studies.

Professor Howard considers that my polemic (*Protest and Survive*) misrepresented his views. I still consider that his letter was open to the reading which I gave it, in most (but not in all) respects. The premises of deterrence theory in which it had been couched (perhaps in an effort to influence authorities who attend to no other premises) are nihilist, and they merited exposure as such. But in attributing to Mr Howard all the sins of deterrence theory—a theory to which he has given only qualified acceptance—I did him an injustice. I can scarcely repair that injustice now, but I can signal, with respect, that he has repaired it himself in an article which marks out his own distaste for deterrence theory (in its reigning versions) and the great distance which lies between it and his own more flexible historical enquiries.

War [Mr Howard quotes from Clausewitz]

> is only a branch of political activity; it is in no sense autonomous. . . It cannot be divorced from political life—and whenever this occurs in our thinking about war, the many links that connect the two elements are destroyed, and we are left with something that is pointless and devoid of sense.

And Mr Howard himself continues:

> When I read the flood of scenarios in strategic journals about first-strike capabilities, counter-force or countervailing strategies, flexible response, escalation dominance and the rest of the postulates of nuclear theology, I ask myself in bewilderment: this war they are describing, *what is it about?* The defense of Western Europe? Access to the Gulf? The protection of Japan? If so, why is this goal not mentioned, and why is the strategy not related to the progress of the conflict in these regions? But if it is not related to this kind of specific object, what are we talking about? Has not the bulk of American thinking been exactly what Clausewitz described—something that, because it is divorced from any political context, is 'pointless and devoid of sense'?
>
> ('On Fighting a Nuclear War', *International Security,* Spring 1981)

Since my first brush with Professor Howard my own acquaintance with the kind of pure deterrence theory which he has identified as 'theology' has become closer. And I must argue that much of the work of its reigning specialists has become intellectually disreputable, and ought not to be supported by any university. Those who have not studied the specialist treatises and periodicals may sample the character of the work in the Winter 1981 number of *Daedalus,* published (alas) by the American Academy of Arts and Sciences, and devoted to 'United States Defense Policy in the 1980s'.

I read this special issue with attention and growing amazement. I found it to be (in the majority of its articles) a barbaric utterance, and in its sum a signal that civilisation is already defeated beyond remedy.

Indeed, this defeat is *assumed,* as a first premise of the discourse. It is assumed that two great blocs are in a state of permanent war (restrained only by something called 'deterrence') and will, forever, remain so. The expertise of the authors—and they were selected for their acknowledged expertise—is contained within an infantile political view of the world, derived, I suppose, from too much early reading of Tolkien's *Lord of the Rings.* The evil kingdom of Mordor lies there, and there it ever will lie, while on our side lies the nice republic of Eriador, inhabited by confused liberal hobbits who are rescued from time to time by the genial white wizardry of Gandalf-figures such as Henry Kissinger, Zbigniew Brzezinski, or Al Haig.

This is an overstatement, for in fact most of the contributors to this issue say little about politics at all. A Manichaean world view is assumed, and the rest is politically null. That is, perhaps, what a top-flight 'defence expert' is: a person with a hole in the head where politics and morality ought to be, who can then get along all the better with moving around the acronyms, in a vocabulary of throw-weight, delivery-systems, megatons and the extrapolation of ever-more-tenuous worst-case scenarios.

'Controlling the escalation process by providing NATO with a wider menu of realistic nuclear options has become an important priority.' That is a sample of the use of English of one of these experts, Mr Richard Burt, whose extremist views as to the abject decline of American military strength were presented extensively in the *New York Times* in the weeks before the late American elections. (He is now one of President Reagan's senior defence advisers.) And another notable expert, Professor Michael Nacht, comes forward proudly as the inventor of a new 'defensive' concept, that of 'pre-emptive deterrence'. Pre-emptive deterrence consists in pre-emptive *aggressive* actions around the world in pursuit of strategic advantage or scarce minerals, raw materials, oil and so forth, and he recommends this brave new concept to the attention of the new United States administration—but in a moderate kind of way, of course, and only when 'US security interests' or 'the intrinsic value of the assets' are important, and, even then, only in 'favourable circumstances'.

It turns out from Professor Nacht's tables that assets with 'intrinsic' or strategic value can be found in most parts of the Third World. That is a sobering reflection. But I have also been puzzling, as a European, to work out how this 'wider menu' of nuclear options might be consumed on this continent, and what 'pre-emptive deterrence' might lead on to here. The view of Europe of several of these distinguished contributors is somewhat hazy. Scholars so high in the world, whose advice is solicited by statesmen and editors, must take large and distant views. One expert notes that–

> Western Europe (like South Korea) amounts geographically to a peninsula projecting out from the Eurasian land mass from which large contingents of military forces can emerge on relatively short notice to invade the peninsula.

The vision informing such sentences merits our attention. The juxtaposition of 'land mass' and 'peninsula' imposes the suggestion that the situation of Western Europe must perforce be precarious. (For the same geo-physical reasons the situation of Florida vis-a-vis the other United States must be precarious in the extreme.) This is the vision of the circumnavigating satellite: from its point of observation, Greenland or the Kola peninsula are more significant than Italy or the two Germanys. The vision excludes all historical or political dimensions: it would be futile to remind the author of two occasions in the past 200 years when large contingents of military force have 'emerged' from the peninsula and invaded the land mass. But the largest of political assumptions has been assumed in the vision itself: the ineluctable opposition of Eriador and Mordor, and the aggressive intent of the latter.

I have indicated matters of style and stance rather than particular arguments. For what we are confronted with–and I am now trying to identify the intellectual credentials of deterrence theory–is not a branch of scholarship but a scholasticism. Like all scholasticisms the practitioners are trapped within the enclosed circularity of their own self-validating logic. Every conclusion is entailed within the theory's premises, although a finely-wrought filigree of logic may be spun between one and the other. And the same premises may give rise to varied and contradictory conclusions, since so much of the exercise is a speculation in futurology which admits of no empirical validation: the matter of the argument deals with linkages, thresholds and ceilings, 'windows of opportunity', the 'balance' of unlike quantities and qualities, alternative perceptions, the 'credibility' of 'postures', the probable and possible outcome of weaponry decisions in ten or twenty or thirty years time.

I do not know whether the academic community realises what an extraordinary intellectual creature co-habits with the high scholarship of American universities. (I do not refer to Russian universities, since this is beyond my knowledge, but I suppose that a blunter, more militaristic, and more segregated, creature co-habits there also.) This creature is increasingly cutting every bridge which might link it with adjacent humanities: with political theory, with history (in all but its military branches), with sociology, with the analysis of culture. It operates on the basis of second-hand and contaminated data, provided in large part by the intelligence services or by the public relations lobbies of the armed forces; and the official secrecy protecting much of its subject-matter inhibits close empirical engagement with the data. The discipline, or pseudo-discipline, attracts indicative funding. It also attracts ambitious men and women who aspire to be advisers to Presidents and who know that if they do not maintain good relations with Defense department officials and the military they will be starved of information and denied an audience for their work.

The more one examines this specialist literature, the more one is driven to ask the same question as Professor Michael Howard has already asked: *'What is it about?'* And what are its methods? The only proof which the theory can offer rests upon an exercise in counter-factual history. Its major procedures are predictive, yet its predictions are of a kind which can never be verified or falsified: they consist, rather, in speculative exercises in futurology, derived from worst-case analysis. These speculations commence (as we have seen) by excluding all variables not related directly to weaponry and strategy. This enables theorists to proceed by attributing a rationality to states which can rarely be found in history: that is, a rational calculation of advantage in the pursuit of self-interest, untroubled by those non-rational surges (of panic or of national self-assertion) which mark the historical record. The predictions also suppose, when they come to 'thresholds' or to menus of 'nuclear options', a fine-tuning between 'posture' and 'perception' which strains any credibility. What if postures are misperceived by the adversary (as they commonly are), or if the alternative strategic premises of the adversaries do not mesh? What if the Russians are playing a different game from the Americans, and each ignores or misunderstands the others' rules? And, finally, this predictive theory can only operate by assuming an accuracy in the delivery of weapons, and a command and control of operations (with supporting communications) which is altogether improbable. This accuracy is neither evinced in history nor in today's world of the helicopter fiasco in Iran. The performance of new weapons like the cruise missiles is acclaimed in the ecstatic terms of the manufacturers' advertising brochures. I will not say that the first cruise missile deployed at a target near Leningrad will in fact turn around and take out Massachusetts. I will only say, as an old soldier, that the claims of boffins and of staff officers for their perfect weapons or their perfect battle-plans only make me yawn. Old soldiers know that the only general who commands both sides on every battlefield is General Ballsup.

There are reasons why this very odd exercise in futurology has acquired some influence. The research and development of new weaponry requires a longer period of forward planning than has ever been known before: ten, fifteen, twenty, and now thirty years. Hence R & D, which is a major *interest* in both blocs, requires a predictive 'science' to justify its inertia and expenditures. And the SALT negotiations consolidated this 'science' and gave to it credibility. Seven years were expended in the fruitless pursuit of SALT II, and during this period many expert minds were employed, on both sides, precisely in the work of predicting consequences, searching for loopholes, and imagining the new weapons and strategies of the adversary. The humane experts of arms control first broke their teeth upon a diet of SALT, and ultimately broke their hearts. But, paradoxically, the SALT negotiations were also the incubator of this inhumane scholasticism, as other minds were tricked, by the continual elaboration of worst-case hypotheses, into the ultra-sophistication of contemporary deterrence theory.

Let us look more closely at two procedures: counter-factual 'proof' and worst-case analysis. Counter-factual history, as an exercise in historical logic, is not necessarily disreputable. But the exercises in this case are trivial. The most commonly-found example, which is now part of everyday political discourse, is that 'deterrence', in the past thirty years, has 'worked', in Europe if not in the rest of the world. The proposition is made: there would have been a major European war, at some point between 1950 and 1980, if it had not been for 'the deterrent'.

Now this is not a stupid proposition. It might be true and it might not; it is a counter-factual proposition which does not admit of proof. And if we allow it some force (as I think we might) it establishes nothing about the future. There are episodes in those years–the Berlin air-lift, the Hungarian insurrection in 1956–which might have occasioned war. This war (we should note) might equally well have been promoted from the West–to reunite Germany or to 'liberate' Eastern Europe–as (in the obligatory scenario of Russian tanks rolling upon the Channel ports) from the East. But this war did not happen. And there is some factual evidence which suggests that 'deterrence' was not the only reason for this. Thus Yugoslavia and Albania succeeded in detaching themselves from the Soviet Union, without recourse to the nuclear 'umbrella', and without war. Given the post-war settlement of Eastern Europe (and I am not apologising for this), there has been no further Soviet expansion upon adjacent non-NATO states: Finland, Austria, or Sweden. Moreover, as Alva Myrdal has argued, there are few territorial or national disputes in contemporary Europe so grave as to be evident occasions for war; and those which remain are found either between states *within* the same alliance (the Greco-Turkish disputes) or in grey areas removed from nuclear threat (the

Yugoslav-Bulgarian dispute about Macedonia). And, finally, if we were to accept the argument that for thirty years the opposed alliances might have had recourse to war if they had not been 'deterred', this affords no proof that nuclear weapons were essential to this 'deterrence', and no proof whatsoever that nuclear weaponry on the present scale of overkill made 'deterrence' more efficient. For what might have deterred the opposing powers from war might have been war itself: that is, 'conventional' war, on a scale as great or greater than World War II–a war which had certain inconvenient and not wholly acceptable attributes. There was, as I recall, no particular appetite in Europe at the end of World War II to commence forthwith upon another. If the appetite at some time in the past thirty years revived, then I wish the counter-factual theorists would do a little serious historical work and show that this was so.

I am only making the obvious point that even counter-factual history must attend scrupulously to evidence, and must take the fullest view of this evidence (in its political, ideological, social and cultural as well as purely strategic aspects) in order to identify motivations and possibilities. That is, this is a problem requiring the full resources of the historical discipline. But the theorists of deterrence foreclose this examination by postulating as a premise exactly what research and analysis alone could find out. It is assumed that the armed forces of the rival blocs stand waiting to overwhelm each other at the first sign of weakness, and would have done so long ago had it not been for the fear of MAD.

This is premise A of deterrence theory, from which the rest of its alphabet follows. Our own weapons are for deterrence; but the weapons of the other side will, or may, be unloosed at the first sign of tactical or strategic advantage. It is not essential to say that they *will* be; to say that they *may* be is sufficient. Worst-case analysis then proceeds (and this is an extraordinary intellectual procedure) by excluding as inadmissable every other kind of evidence as to political, social and cultural reality. In monomanic fashion it applies its forecasting to this one thing: might there possibly be, now or at some future date, a point of tactical or strategic disadvantage, a weak link in the system of balance, or confusion of posture and perception, which would permit the adversary to strike? And it is assumed (for the purposes of this theory) that the adversary must at all times be malevolent, amoral, opportunist, and possessed by no motivations other than absolute hostility.

I can think of no reputable discipline which proceeds by such methods. Of course, any discipline–economics, demography or criminology–narrows its vision to certain phenomena only, and excludes the irrelevant. But it does not then–or it should not–smuggle back into its premises arbitrary assumptions as to the excluded phenomena. If criminology were to assume, as its first premise, that society is divided into two parties: the police and the law on one side, and all other citizens on the other: and, further, that all citizens will always seek opportunities to commit murder unless effectively deterred: then the theory would commence as apologetics for a police-state, with a gibbet at every cross-roads. Criminology would then, by imagining murderers everywhere, actually provoke a state of conflict and induce more murders (judicial or other), just as deterrence theory is inducing nuclear war.

The elementary notion of deterrence–the cave men with their clubs, or a few ICBMs on each side–has a certain common-sense plausibility. It has even sometimes worked. But deterrence theory, in its scholastic or vulgar political expression, has long parted company with common-sense. By excluding all other phenomena, except the worst case, from view it offers, always, weaponry as a *substitute* for the diplomatic or political resolution of differences. It freezes all political process and, increasingly, on both sides, constricts even cultural and intellectual exchanges within the same ideological parameters.

More than this. Worst-case analysis (by excluding the possibility of any better cases, and by refusing to consider any measures which might bring the better about) actually *induces* the worst case to arise. This is the entire record of weaponry, the pursuit of advantage, of the past two decades: the inducement of one worst case after another. Deterrence theory, by accelerating R & D and by summoning new weapons forward, is the ideological drive of addiction. In this ideological role it is indeed an operative force. Like an addictive drug, it induces euphoria, inhibits the perception of manifest consequences, and excuses the inexcusable.

It is odd. The number of influential 'defence experts' in both blocs probably only amounts to a few hundred. All around these rocky islets there is a sea of authentic scholarship—historical, political, sociological, and in military or peace studies. The scholars take little notice of the increasingly abstruse, acronymic and hermetic discourse which goes on on the islets; they think of these practitioners, perhaps, as rather well-funded freaks; those who have looked into the defence literature know that it is very weird.

Yet this intellectually-vacant pseudo-discipline carries greater influence upon the outcome of civilisation, and commands vaster human resources, than any intellectual exercise in history. Examine the history of the MX missile project. This originated in a classic exercise of deterrence theory, or worst-case alarmism. Eminent practitioners signalled that the increasing accuracy of Soviet ICBM delivery systems placed the United States land-based Minutemen silos at risk; the adversary was being offered a 'window of opportunity', and with a first strike could 'take out' every one of these silos. This afforded the theoretical rationale for the most expensive construction project in all history, the MX mobile 'shell-game', with its tracks and roadways which would have occupied half of the states of Utah and Nevada. The operative pressures behind this project were ideological and economic—in particular the vast pickings afforded to the arms lobby at a time of recession. But it was this paper-thin piece of worst-case analysis which provided the theoretical rationale.

Even as worst-case analysis it was badly flawed. United States nuclear menace stands on three legs: land, air and sea: and of these, only the first leg could possibly be imperilled by this fictional first strike. No Soviet command, however malevolent, could possibly unloose such a first strike in the expectation of remaining immune from an air- and sea-launched response. Moreover, as US inter-service rivalries have built up—promoting alternative ventures—and as

President Reagan's Republican friends in Utah and Nevada have become restive, it suddenly turns out that the original analysis was absurd also. The Soviet ICBMs are not as accurate as the worst-case predicted; no first strike could possibly take out more than a proportion of the Minutemen silos. New learned articles are now being published, and the theory is undergoing revision.

How could it have come about that something above fifty billion dollars could be authorised to be spent upon a flawed argument based upon worst-case projections in a disreputable discipline? Or let us take another case. The ceaseless pursuit of advantage, rationalised by the worst-case analysis of both sides, has led to the present missile crisis in Europe: the build-up of SS-20s, the summoning on of cruise and Pershing II missiles. It is evident that neither weapon will contribute to European security: on the contrary, Europeans are feeling decidedly insecure.

Both sides justify their measures in terms of 'balance' within deterrence theory. The Soviet apologists argue that they are only modernising and replacing their SS-4s and SS-5s, and matching the (largely sea- and air-borne) forces of the West. What they disguise is that the modernised weapons are both more accurate, and are mobile and hence more difficult to target. The Western theorists are even less plausible. They designate as intermediate or theatre weapons missiles which can reach far behind Moscow and which can destroy the most densely-populated and densely-industrialised territory of their adversary: what may be intermediate to the Pentagon is as immediate as some five minutes flight to the Kremlin. In Russian perception these new missiles are not intermediate at all, but are forward-based United States strategic missiles which decisively tilt the 'balance' against them. If deterrence theory had been an objective discipline, one would have supposed that this self-evident difference in perception—what Sir Martin Ryle has called 'geographical asymmetry'—would have been registered impartially at the outset of the discussion. But, in my reading of the literature, this manifest point was universally overlooked; or was noted only by those distinguished advisers and arms controllers of an older generation who have been pushed out into the margins of protest.

Deterrence theory, then, has long parted company with science and has become the ideological lubricant of the arms race. Its theories can be turned to use by the arms manufacturers or by military lobbies; or they can be brought in afterwards to justify anything. To be anything more than that, it would have to be fleshed out with some empirical substance; it would have to engage with the full historical process; and, at the end of all its worst-case predictions, it would have to envisage some way forward to an ultimate better case—to proffer some little advice as to policies which might possibly advance the better and forestall the cumulative worst.

And how do deterrence theorists suppose that this race will ever end? Short of a final nuclear war, I suppose that there are these alternative scenarios. Soviet ideologists may suppose that, in the end, Western capitalism will collapse, with conjoint recession and inflation, shortage of energy resources, internal insurrection and revolt throughout the Third World. Western ideologists suppose that the Soviet economy will collapse under the burden of increasing arms allocations, with internal nationalist and dissident movements, and with insurrection or near-insurrection throughout Eastern Europe.

But these theorists need only cross the corridor and knock on the doors of their colleagues in History, Politics or Sociology, to learn that these scenarios might provide, precisely, the moment of the worst case of all. Each of these developments would bring the continent, and ultimately the world itself, into the greatest peril. Each would provide the conditions, not for the peaceful reunification of Europe, but the rise of panic-stricken, authoritarian regimes, tempted to maintain the discipline of their peoples by recourse to military adventures. The break-down of East or West, in a situation of massive military confrontation, would tend to precipitate the resolution of war. And, indeed, already the military and political elites, both East and West, who are now sensing gathering difficulties within their own systems, are showing that they need the Cold War—they need to put not only their missiles but also their ideology and security systems into good repair—as a means of internal social control.

In doing this, these elites find deterrence theory to be of increasing service. We pass into a new, exalted stage where deterrence theory becomes the astrology of the nuclear age. It is a peculiar situation. In the case of internal ideological systems, the public normally have some experiential means of checking the ideology's veracity. Thus monetarism may appear as a superbly-logical system, but we still know what prices are in the shops, which of our neighbours are unemployed, and who has gone bankrupt. But in the case of deterrence theory, the ideologists control both the intellectual system and the information input. None of us has ever seen an SS-20, nor can we count their numbers; none of us can check out the throw-weight or circular error probable of a Trident missile. We have no experiential means of critique whatsoever. The information itself is pre-processed within an ideological matrix (the intelligence services) and is presented with intent to prejudice.

This presents us with an extraordinary problem of epistemology. The sciences and social sciences alike have been subjected to epistemological criticism in past decades, and have sometimes been given a rough passage. But deterrence theory cannot bear any scrutiny of this kind at all. It is well-established that President Kennedy was carried to power by an alarmed electorate who had been informed (by him) of a 'missile gap', in the Soviet Union's favour—a gap which was wholly fictional. President Reagan has now been swept to power upon a similar tide of prejudicial information and fictions. An academic discipline which has failed to challenge, frontally, these major exercises in public deception—which has covered up for them, or even provided the trumpeters and drummers for the whole mendacious exercise—a discipline which has left it to a handful of honourable dissenters, outsiders, and amateurs to contest, with small resources, the well-funded lies of State—such a discipline must stand self-condemned.

Militarisation in the advanced world today has these contradictory features. It is distinguished by the very low visibility of some of its activities and the high visibility of others. The actual military presence, in most parts of Western although not in all parts of Eastern Europe, is very low. This is not a time, as were the Jingo days before World War I or as was Hitler's Germany in the late 1930s, of ostentatious parades, rallies, tattoos, and the ubiquitous recruiting sergeant. The actual weapons are invisible, at Grand Forks, North Dakota, or on the Kola peninsula, or at sea. The attendant communications and security operations–although these may be our neighbours–are kept invisible behind a screen of Official Secrecy. The militarisation of nuclear weapons warfare is science- and capital-intensive; it does not require a huge uniformed labour force, nor does it necessitate conscription or the draft. The growing retinue of 'deterrence' is more likely to be in mufti: in manufacture, research and development; we may exchange small-talk with them in the university common-room–easy-going, civilian, decidedly-unmilitary types.

But at the same time militarisation as ideology has an increasingly sensational visibility. It is presented to us, on television, in the speeches of politicians, as the threat of the Other: the Backfire bomber, the SS-20, the hordes of Soviet tanks. It is necessary–and on both sides–to make the public's flesh creep in order to justify the expense and the manifest risks of 'our deterrents'. With the break-up of the Cominform, and the weakness and disarray of Western Communist movements, no-one is much impressed today with the story-line of the first Cold War: the threat from within. (This story-line still works, to more effect, in the East.) What then must be imprinted upon the public mind is the escalating threat from without. Deterrence theory is elevated to the Chair of Propaganda. Professor Caspar Weinberger orders the neutron bomb; but at the same time he orders a sensational account of the build-up of Soviet weaponry to be sent on to Western Europe, to make plain the way of the bomb.

The other contradiction is this. None of these weapons–*none* of them–can ever be used, except for the final holocaust. As Mr Kennan has told us: 'The nuclear bomb is the most useless weapon ever invented. . . It is not even an effective defense against itself.' There is an existing state of threat: but to add and add to that threat is, in military terms, futile. Given the initial equilibrium of MAD, each additional weapon has been useless. They might as well not exist. The significance of these weapons is symbolic only.

I say 'symbolic only'; but as a social historian I have often offered the view that symbolism is a profoundly important constituent of historical process. Symbolic confrontations precede and accompany confrontations by force. They are often also a means of sublimating or displacing confrontations of force, with real and material consequences. A contest for 'face' may, in its outcome, confirm or call in question the authority of the rulers. The rituals of State, the public execution, the popular demonstration—all carry symbolic force; they may consolidate the assured hegemony of the rulers or they may bring it into disrepute with numbers and ridicule. Symbolism is not a mere colour added to the facts of power: it is an element of societal power in its own right.

New generations of nuclear missiles are counters in a contest for 'face'. But they are not less dangerous because they are only symbolic. They are carriers of the most barbarous symbolism in history. They spell out to our human neighbours that we are ready, at any instant, to annihilate them, and that we are perfecting the means. They spell out also the rejection of alternative means of resolving differences. That is why—as symbols—they must be rejected. As weapons they are useless, except for the final event; they exist, today, only as symbols of barbaric menace and of human self-defeat. And the consequence of the first rejections of these symbols will, in its turn, be of profound and hopeful symbolic significance. It will demystify the theory of deterrence, and symbolise the pursuit of alternative solutions.

What should properly command our attention today is not the theory of deterrence—whether or not it may have 'worked' on this or that occasion—but the social and political *consequences* of its working over two decades. From one aspect these consequences are merely absurd. Anthropologists will be familiar with the potlach—the ritual and ceremonial destruction, by primitive peoples, of their surplus food and resources. From this aspect, the nuclear arms race is nothing but a gigantic potlach. From another aspect, matters are perilous. It is not only that these weapons do actually exist; their function may be as symbols, but they remain there, on their launch-pads, instantly ready. The weapons themselves have been consumed in no potlach, only the human resources have been consumed. And there are now new and devilish strategies which propose that they might actually, in 'limited' ways, be used. Insane as it is, deterrence theory could, like other insanities, be self-fulfilling. By conditioning military and political elites, on both sides, to act in accord with the first premise of adversary posture—to seek ceaselessly for advantage and to expect annihilating attack upon the first sign of weakness—it could tempt one side (if a manifest advantage should arise) to behave as theory prescribes, and to seize the opportunity for a pre-emptive strike. And what would the war, then, have been *about*? It would have been about fulfilling a theorem in deterrence theory.

But the greater peril does not lie here. It lies in the consequences of a course of action which has frozen diplomatic and political process and has continually postponed the making of peace. Deterrence theory proceeded by excluding as irrelevant all that was extraneous to weaponry. But no theory can prohibit economic and political process from going on. Through these two decades, frustrated aggression has fed back into the opposed societies; the barbarous symbolism of weaponry has corrupted the opposed cultures; the real and material bases of the weapons-systems—the military-industrial complexes of both sides—have enlarged and consolidated their political influence; militarism has increased its retinue of civilian retainers; the security services and security-minded ideologies have been strengthened; the Cold War has consolidated itself, not as between both parties, but as an indigenous *interest* within each one. This is a proper—and urgent—matter for scientific, economic, and political enquiry.

Deterrence theory proposed a stationary state: that of MAD. But history knows no stationary states. As deterrence presides, both parties change; they become addicted; they become uglier and more barbarous in their postures and gestures. They turn into societies whose production, ideology, and research is increasingly directed towards war. 'Deterrence' enters deeply into the structure, the economy, and the culture of both blocs. This is the reason—and not this or that advantage in weaponry, or political contingency—why nuclear war is probable within our lifetimes. It is not just that we are preparing for war; we are preparing ourselves to be *the kind of societies which go to war.*

I doubt if there is any way out, although increasing numbers are searching for it. Since the weapons are useless, and function only as symbols, we could commence to behave as if they do not exist. We could then resume every possible mode of discourse—inter-personal, scholarly, diplomatic—designed to break up the unnatural opposition of the blocs, whose adversary posture lies behind the entire operation. But the melding of the blocs can never take place upon terms of the 'victory' of one side over the other; it must be done, not by the states, but in some part *against* the states of both sides. This means that we cannot leave the work to statesmen, nor to the functionaries of states, to do on their own. Political and military leaders, by the very nature of politics and military service, are the last to abandon adversary postures; and as soon as they do so, they are accused by their opponents of complicity with the adversary.

The work would have to be done, at least in the first stages, *beneath* the level of states. There would have to be an unprecedented investment of the voluntary resources of ordinary citizens in threading a new skein of peace. In this work scholars and intellectuals would find that they had particular duties, both because of their specialist skills and opportunities, and because of the universal humane claims of their sciences and arts. I am not inviting them to 'go into politics'. I am saying that they must go *ahead* of politics, and attempt to put European culture back together: or all politics and all culture will cease.

THE END OF THE LINE

Nigel Calder is a most able practitioner in the 'high popularisation' of science and technology, and his work demands respectful attention.[1] *Nuclear Nightmares* is an instant party-stopper, and a book to press into the hands of your flippant nephew or giddy niece. More seriously, it deserves a general readership, as a brisk and informed run-through of the technological and strategic infrastructure of World War III.

What Calder does is to show the massing of weaponry, its sophistication, the logic of interlocking strategies, and the several points where 'deterrence' may pass swiftly into war in a compulsive process in which peoples and governments have become 'the servants rather than the masters of that which they have created'. Those words are George Kennan's, and Calder's book might be taken as a densely-observed extended illustration of Kennan's more general summary:

> . . . that immensely disturbing and tragic situation in which we find ourselves today: this anxious competition in the development of new armaments: this blind dehumanization of the prospective adversary; this systematic distortion of the adversary's motivation and intentions; this steady displacement of political considerations by military ones in the calculations of statesmanship; in short, this dreadful militarization of the entire East-West relationship in concept, in rhetoric, and in assumption, which is the commanding feature–endlessly dangerous, endlessly discouraging–of this present unhappy day.[2]

Yet I cannot disguise my view that Calder's book, as well as others in this growing genre, are also symptoms of this

This article first appeared in *The Bulletin of the Atomic Scientists,* January 1981, Vol. 37 no. 1.

unhappy day. They neither challenge nor, in any fundamental way, do they diagnose. Rather, they exhibit precisely 'the steady displacement of political considerations by military ones'. The sophistication of the technological reportage masks an inadequacy in the treatment of political process. The brisk bravura of Calder's style presses always toward the exotic and exclamatory mode of science fiction: it has no terms of graver meditation on our predicament, and no space for the measured analysis of the actions of states. Louis René Beres's *Apocalypse* prompts the same reflections: carrying some useful information, and also more positive proposals than Calder does, its analysis of political process is nevertheless sadly defective.[3]

What happens in these cases is that analysis is forced, unwittingly, into the parameters of a self-fulfilling argument. Founded upon the evidence of weapons and strategies, whose rationale is always that of 'deterrence', there is no space in which the validity of any alternative rationale can be allowed or examined. We are inside the rationale which has led us to this unhappy day, and which will shortly lead us to worse, and we can never get out. Whether the balance of evidence or perception is tilted towards the West or East (how many systems, what worst case expectations?), the analysis is confined *within the same parameters:* that is, within the leap-frog logic of deterrence. Within this logic the hawks of each side feed to each other arms and provocations. They strive for 'parity' envisage 'gaps' and 'windows of opportunity'. Through never-ending negotiations at the highest level they adumbrate elaborate devices of 'control' and trade-off, which their clever games-players then seek to evade or to turn to new advantage, and thus generate more thrust in the course toward collision.

Operating within such parameters, Calder, at the end simply gives up. Disarmament conferences are dismissed as the background croaking of frogs beside the silos at Grand Forks; any reversal of the collision-course could be more dangerous than going on as we are. Beres, willing himself to be more positive, offers new proposals for arms control negotiators at the very topmost level, some of which are neat and deserve attention. Yet none of these proposals will be worth a dime unless there are profound, worldwide modifications in public consciousness, which bring their thrust to bear in the realm of active, operative *politics*—modifications for which the paradigm of deterrence offers no terms.

I find that many North Americans these days are profoundly pessimistic about any such utopian expectations: the well-informed are despairing, and they hope, at the best, only to slow down the leapfrog logic. Europeans have become in the past year a shade more desperate, and they are in increasing numbers despairing of the logic of deterrence. They are looking outside the old parameters of 'balance' to the long-neglected processes of political discourse and cultural expression. Across the widening Atlantic we send you greetings, but also our storm signals of despair.

Arguments founded upon weaponry and strategy are enclosed within a determinism whose outcome must be war. All that doves can do within these parameters is check or decelerate a thrust which (next month, next year, next crisis, next election) accelerates once more. If there is anywhere any hope, we must search for it outside this determinism. I will proceed by defining certain areas of concern which Calder's book, and others of this genre, do *not* discuss. Those I select (for there are many others) are:

- —the ultimate location of the upward 'creep' of weaponry;
- —ideological problems relating to the control and manipulation of information; and
- —a particular case of the politics of weaponry, illustrated by NATO 'modernization'.

Weapons do not, as yet, invent and make themselves. There is a human decision to make them. Who takes such decisions? How?

This is a question more important than those of throw-weight or circular error probable, yet it is assumed unanalysed in deterrence theory. From the time of Eisenhower and Khrushchev, the leaders of the superpowers have shrugged off personal responsibility.[4] But so also have some of the highest scientific and even military advisers to these leaders. I need not mention the distinguished line of arms control scientific and defence advisers to US administrations who have candidly signalled their profound disagreements with the decisions of government. In the Soviet Union, blanket official secrecy makes the record less clear: we must go back as far as Khrushchev's memoirs for a similar account of the rejection of prime scientific advice, in the encounters between Khrushchev and Andrei Sakharov.

In Britain the Official Secrets Acts are so heavy that we learn a little of the process only some years after the event, and then only from advisers so eminent that they are immune from prosecution. Three notable cases can be cited from 1979 to 1980: Lord Louis Mountbatten, Lord Zuckerman, and Field Marshall Lord Carver. Mountbatten, in a concise and humane speech delivered at Strasbourg two months before his murder, signalled his extreme anxiety at the nuclear arms race and indicated the specific advice he had given, when Commander-in-Chief of the British General Staff, against any strategy which entertained the possibility of limited or theatre nuclear war.[5] Carver, another outgoing Commander-in-Chief, and a conventional proponent of NATO deterrence theory, has signalled in a succession of interviews and letters to *The Times* his long-standing opposition to an independent British nuclear weapons system. Zuckerman, who was Chief Scientific Adviser to the British Government from 1964 to 1971, has surveyed, in a lecture of outstanding importance, the record of two decades in which 'the views of the Killians, the Wiesners, the Kistiakowskys, the Yorks'–and (by implication) the Zuckermans–were consistently overruled.[6]

We are faced with an extraordinary situation, although not a situation for which a historian is altogether unprepared. Not only the nominal leaders of states but also their chief scientific advisers and chiefs of general staff disclaim responsibility for the most central decisions of state policy. All gesture toward an ulterior process to which they themselves became captive. It was Eisenhower who warned of the 'danger that public policy could itself become the captive of a scientific-technological elite'. Zuckerman, the scientist, passes the buck down the line to technology. The 'military chiefs, who by convention are the official advisers on national security, merely serve as a channel through which the men in the laboratories transmit their views', and 'chief scientific advisers have proved to be no match for the laboratory technicians':

> The men in the nuclear weapons laboratories of both sides have succeeded in creating a world with an irrational foundation, on which a new set of political realities has in turn had to be built. They have become the alchemists of our times, working in secret ways which cannot be divulged, casting spells which embrace us all.

We have at last identified the human agent of our doom, concealed within a secret laboratory, casting malevolent spells. And this brings us close to the findings of experts on arms control who have identified the ulterior thrust towards weapons innovation in such terms as technology creep.[7] Undoubtedly this directs us to a significant moment of process, which appears to its own actors in this way. Yet there is still something unexplained. For this traces the most significant tendency of our times to a source, either in a laboratory conspiracy, or in an inexorable technological determinism of a kind for which historians (or, I should say, historians whom I consider to be reputable) do not find any historical precedent. That is, some vulgar practitioners of determinism apart, historians do not find that technology (or inventors), unaided, created industrialisation or capitalism or imperialism. Nor can technology creep, unaided, bring us to extermination. Historians find, rather, a collocation of mutually-supportive forces–political, ideological, institutional, economic–which give rise to process, or to the event. And each of these forces exists only within the medium of human agency.

I see no reason why this historical finding must now undergo drastic revision. But this need not lead us toward any optimistic conclusions. We may be led to an even more pessimistic finding: that technology creep is indeed supplemented by a host of collateral and mutually supportive forces which, taken as a set, constitute the process which has led us to Kennan's 'this present unhappy day'. And if we read Zuckerman with care, we find that the men in the laboratories did not do all this alone. They also 'knew how to respond to the mood of the country, how to capture the attention of the media, how to stir the hearts of generals. They have been adept. . . in creating the climate within which political chiefs have to operate'.[8]

The cast has now become larger: it takes in public opinion, the media, the military, the politicians. In sum:

- –the weapons systems–and their 'laboratory' technicians, lobbyists and public relations operators–attract a large concentration of the resources and scientific skills of the host society and are then transformed into huge inertial forces within that society, whether bureaucratic or private in expression;
- –they are interlocked with the government bureaucracy (exchange of personnel with Defence ministries and with Party bureaucracy, and so forth), and become adept at lobbying in the media and in the organs of the state;
- –there is generated around them a large supportive and protective security and policing apparatus, which, in its turn, enhances the control of information and the inhibition of opposition, and which actively furthers the crystallisation of a supportive ideology.

Politicians then rise in influence from the weapons system and security apparatus themselves (Brezhnev, Haig). As in all long-term historical processes–and imperialisms provide clear examples–now one and now another of the collateral forces may attain dominance: now the 'alchemists in the laboratories', now the generals, now the media, now the politicians, may appear to be calling the tune. But this is only as it seems to the actors at a particular moment within the process, for in truth, alchemists, politicians, generals and ideologists are all part of one set. Technology can creep only because ideology is creeping alongside it and because politicians are creeping away from any decisive control. And behind the politicians is the pressure of those hundreds of thousands of electors who 'are making their livings doing things which were promoted years before by their political predecessors. It is the past which imbues the arms race with its inner momentum'.[9]

That is a pessimistic conclusion indeed.[10] It leads reflective persons within the system to suppose that there may be only one remote possibility of staving off the end. By some wizardry at the highest level of diplomatic engineering between the superpowers—SALT XIII?—the plug will at the last moment be pulled, and the waters of nuclear menace will drain out of the rival baths just before they overflow onto the floor of the world. This most momentous political action will be taken, by the leaders of states and their advisers, without any of the normal preliminaries of general political agitation and discourse. It is supposed that the very same political forces which have made these insane structures will suddenly unmake them; the weapons-systems and their political and security support-systems will de-weaponise themselves.

This will not happen. And what this analysis should indicate is that it is precisely at the top of both opposed societies that agreement to de-escalate is *most* impossible. It is here that inertia and 'creep' have their uncontested reign. It is here that the advice of scientists and even of rational military minds is jammed by a concatenation of competing interests and bureaucracies. It is here that the maintenance of cold war becomes an actual *interest*, and an instrument of policy in the subjection and control of client states, in the legitimation of other kinds of adventure, and in the suppression of dissent. It is here that the futile exercises of 'balance', of contests for 'face', of 'posture', of endlessly protracted negotiations about minutiae, and of worst-case hypotheses, govern every encounter.

The conclusion is evident. If we are to develop a counter-thrust to the inertia of the weapons-systems, then we must do this first of all, not at the top, but at the bottom, in the middle, and on the margins of both opposed state structures. Only here is there space for the insertion of any rationality. We can destabilise the weapons-systems only from below. The means must include those of political discourse and agitation; of lateral exchanges of many kinds between the middle ranges of society in the opposed blocs; of detaching client states from their dependency on either bloc and adding to the sum of influence of non-aligned powers; of pressing measures of conversion to peaceful production within the weapons-system itself,[11] and of contesting, with every surviving resource of our culture, the enforcement of security and of information control.

I have written: 'with every *surviving* resource of our culture'. But survival can no longer be assumed. Calder, Beres and other writers in this genre carry warnings about the dangers of nuclear terrorism.[12] The point should be taken, although it is low on the list of the most probable occasions of disaster. What they say very much less about is the danger that the weapons states will themselves become terrorist, and turn their terror against their own peoples.

The evidence is disquieting. The essential information about weapons and strategy (without which no democratic counterforce can possibly be mounted) already comes through to us from only a few channels. The Soviet Union and its client states are governed by the strictest rules of military secrecy. Persons employed at any level in the weapons-systems must renounce travel (for holiday or other purposes) to the West, unless under exceptional and authorised conditions. Similar controls are enforced in several Western states. While public opinion in the Soviet Union and in Eastern Europe is anxious about weaponry and war (and, in the most general sense, is 'peace loving'), the level of information available to citizens on weaponry and strategy is very low. There is almost no public controversy about what options are available to their own statesmen; even the names of weapons (SS-6, SS-20, the Backfire bomber) are unknown.[13]

In Britain the Official Secrets Acts operate with a rigour which surprises many Americans. Even members of successive British cabinets were not informed of the Chevaline programme for the sophistication of the Polaris warhead—a programme which was pressed forward over a period of nearly ten years, at a cost of £1,000 million, without budget sanction and without any mention in the House of Commons.

What is even less widely known in the United States is that the last British government, under the Labour Party, mounted a full state prosecution, based on the Official Secrets Acts, of an ex-corporal who had divulged some low level and very stale information about signals interception to two radical investigative journalists. (They also were prosecuted–not for publishing but simply for *listening* to 'secrets'.) This prosecution, the 'ABC trial' of 1978, was pressed forward by the Security Services, and was accompanied by devices to fiddle or 'vet' the ancient and much-lauded safeguard of British liberties, the jury system.[14]

Margaret Thatcher's Conservative government, shortly after entering into power in 1979, rushed forward a new Official Information Bill. This measure, designed by Security, was heralded by a public relations lobby, presenting it as a rationalising and lenient revision of the law. On inspection–and only after the Bill had been steered by Lord Hailsham through the House of Lords–it was found to be the most draconian measure of thought-control presented to the British legislature since 1820. New clauses were aimed directly at journalists and at peace researchers, enabling Security to break open their offices and files; and if researchers had accumulated materials, *from legitimate open public sources,* which, when pieced together like a jigsaw, revealed an 'official secret', then they were liable to prosecution. An official secret in Britain has been defined as any information on the operations of the state which the state itself has not officially released.

Thatcher's Bill was aborted, in the face of opposition. We can expect a 'reformed' Bill to be re-introduced at some time, although the existing Acts are heavy enough. In the past year some very effective investigative journalism has been going on, notably by Duncan Campbell (one of the defendants in the ABC trial) in the *New Statesman,* which has revealed, among other things, the large extent of telephone tapping and surveillance of British citizens, and the fact that the United States has some four or five times more military bases and installations in Britain than has ever been admitted to the British Parliament. There has also been a 'leakage' of regional Civil Defence contingency plans, which include measures for the internment or execution in the event of war of suspected seditionists. British Security is now itching for a spectacular and successful State trial.

The object of these operations is, of course, not to conceal information from an enemy, but to conceal it from their own citizens. Sometimes, as Zuckerman has noted, 'the rules of official secrecy are exploited, not because of the need for security, but to promote partisan policies' as between competing interests within the state bureaucracies. More generally it is part of the overall exercise in manipulating domestic public opinion. I find these political developments to be greatly more threatening than are scenarios of nuclear terrorism or of war by accident through a snarled computer. The essential precondition to any counterthrust to the inertia of the weapons-systems must be the ever-wider communication of fuller and more objective information about these systems.

In the European Nuclear Disarmament (END) movement we are laying increasing stress on *lateral* communication, on transcontinental (as well as transatlantic) exchanges between specialist groups: universities, scientists, doctors, religious bodies or trade unions. We owe, and the entire world owes, a debt of gratitude to those members of the US scientific, intellectual and arms control community who have steadily held open the channels of information and communication for so many years. They have been the prime providers of whatever information the world now has. The significance of this work is too great to be measured.

Among so many scenarios of the occasions of nuclear war, there is a failure to discuss an actual, immediate and possible occasion of war going on beneath our noses. I refer to the NATO decision to 'modernise' its nuclear armoury.[15]

What so many overlook is that these assumptions pre-empt examination of the most far-reaching political issues, now coming to occupy the centre of European discourse. There have emerged, not two but *three* opposed perceptions of the situation:

–the United States plus NATO perception;

–the Soviet perception; and

–a growing European perception, hostile to both.

I need not rehearse the official NATO view here. In this view, which emerged not in common West European perception but from within the defence bureaucracies of NATO powers, a menacing imbalance or gap was discovered in the

European theatre. Its agents were identified as the Soviet SS-20 missiles and Backfire bombers. It was necessary to match these with Pershing IIs in West Germany and with cruise missiles across the Western board.

The other side of the coin of Official Secrecy is that all information on defence matters is Official Information: that is, it is served up to the public ready-cooked, with ideological dressing, on an official plate. The defence correspondents of the media duly attended Official Briefings and handed these on. Public opinion was manufactured in these ways: the American public was informed that Europeans were crying out for cruise missiles, the European public was informed that the United States insisted upon sending them, and both were informed that NATO was working in the best interests of all.

In an obliterating and highly orchestrated propaganda campaign (funded out of our own taxes) the NATO re-definitions were imposed.[16] It suddenly appeared that, in this European theatre, only ground-launched missiles might be counted; sea-launched missiles might not. The British government issued an official White Paper of astounding mendacity, in which Poseidon, Polaris and countless lesser delivery systems simply disappeared.[17] Pentagon charts, fed into the Western media immediately prior to the NATO decision (at Brussels, December 12, 1979), did much the same.[18]

The television obligingly supplied rushes of monstrous carrier-mounted SS-20s crashing through bushes in their advance upon the Free West. Expert SLOBS (Silver-Lipped Operators of Bullshit) perfected new means of moral lobotomy upon the public: normative and moralistic attributions entered into the very vocabulary of weapons technology, so that menacing missiles of similar destructive power became 'monsters' (if Soviet) and 'deterrents' (if NATO). Thus the pre-packaged NATO perception.

In Soviet perception the notion of this European theatre is a NATO invention, and probably a Pentagon trick. Since cruise and Pershing II missiles are to be owned and operated by US personnel, these are seen as forward-based US *strategic* missiles which reach some 500 miles deeper into

Russia than do the F-111 and the Vulcan–and, indeed, take Moscow and Kiev within their arc. Both missiles are highly accurate, but the Pershing II is speedy also, and can hit targets in Western Russia in anything between four and ten minutes from launch.

Taken together with US Presidential Directive 59, it is now possible to see the Soviet nightmare. Pershing IIs will make a pre-emptive strike, in five minutes flat, taking out Western Russian ICBM silos and, at the same time, an Alaskan-based strike will take out ICBMs in Asiatic Russia. The cruise missiles will saunter along behind, smelling their way over the terrain, and take out control, communications and political centres, as well as half the Russian population. Apart from the few surviving ICBMs, 'the only response open to the Russians would be the launching of their own medium-range missiles against the NATO European allies'.[19] No doubt the opportunity would be taken.

My quotation is from the distinguished East German scientist, Robert Havemann. And it may be necessary to assure Western readers that, so far from being anyone's stooge or apologist, Professor Havemann is an outstanding defender of civil liberties (what Westerners call 'a dissident'), who has been pushed around and held under house arrest by the oafish East German security police for several years.

That Havemann should issue this grave warning is a matter to take into grave account. For what he makes clear is that NATO weapons modernisation is nothing less than a slow-playing Cuban missile crisis in reverse. Putting Pershing IIs in West Germany is an exact analogy with Khrushchev's freighters steaming toward Cuba. Seen in this light, the response of the Soviet political leaders has been rather cooler than that of President Kennedy. Brezhnev's finger has not yet moved toward the button. There are still two years for Western second thoughts, and perhaps for Soviet concessions on the SS-20. But Havemann warns us that these will be very dangerous years: 'How long can the Soviet Union simply observe this process of preparation for a sudden attack which threatens its very existence? Can they afford. . . simply to watch passively?'

I am not quite sure how the third, European, perception

so suddenly emerged, although we did something about it ourselves. It is this. We are pig-in-the-middle while an interminable and threatening argument between born-again Christians and still-born Marxists goes on above our heads. Today there are supposed to be superpower negotiations (or preliminaries to preliminaries to negotiations) going on about European theatre weapons–a matter which could scarcely concern us more–and there is no European seat at the table.

US scenarios for a limited war in the European theatre do not amuse us: this is where we happen to live. And where we will very certainly die in any nuclear exchange (however 'limited'), since, whichever superpower claims itself as the scorched and radiation-stricken 'winner', all of Europe will certainly be devastated. We are clear also that the first consequence of the importation of cruise missiles will be even denser Soviet targeting plans on the recipient nations.[20] Already England's still green but not-so-pleasant land may carry a greater density of nuclear weapons-launching bases (airfields, submarine depots) and ancillary military installations than any part of the world.[21] We are not amused by parliamentary assurances that missiles, owned and operated by foreign personnel, will only be launched after 'consultation' and in our national interests.

Other matters also have become clear. One is the tendency for both military alliances–NATO and the Warsaw Pact–to become instruments of superpower political control, reducing the lesser states to abject cliency. This is as true in the West as in the East of Europe. Another is the fact that Eastern and Western Europeans live in the same theatre, are subject to the same menace, and are rediscovering common interests. It has occurred to us that if the West leaned a little less heavily upon the East with missiles, then self-activating democratic processes (as in Poland) might have greater room to move; and that the Western peace movement and the Eastern movement for democratisation might make common cause.

The new movement for European nuclear disarmament has grown with astonishing rapidity. It commenced, long before December 1979, with the refusal of Norway and Denmark even to entertain cruise missiles. In Norway the movement was initiated by a few concerned citizens who organised a telephone-bombardment of the Norwegian Assembly. It moved on to Holland, where in a remarkably successful alliance which stretched from the Dutch churches through the Radical and Labour parties to the far left, a campaign was initiated—of petitioning, of discussion, and of torch-light processions. This culminated in the defeat of the Dutch government in the Assembly on December 11, 1979—the day before the NATO meeting. Under such pressures both Holland and Belgium have delayed their decision on the missiles.

The British hibernated all through that winter, while the falling leaves of 'official information' choked up all entries to their burrows. But, coming out into the daylight in the spring of 1980, they looked around at the changing scene and did not like it. There has been a swift change in perception. Anti-missile groups have sprung up across the country, thickest in East Anglia and Berkshire (around the nominated missile harbours). The long-standing Campaign for Nuclear Disarmament has been rejuvenated. Trade unions and the Labour Party have adopted uncompromising policies rejecting both the cruise and Trident missiles. It is becoming increasingly unlikely that the introduction of cruise missiles into Britain is politically viable. And if Thatcher introduces them, Michael Foot—the newly-elected Leader of the Labour Party—has promised that he will send them back.

The contribution of European Nuclear Disarmament to this has been one of putting together movements and individuals, in East as well as West Europe, behind a common platform and a common strategy. Our Appeal was issued in April 1980 over a transcontinental list of signatories. It calls upon NATO and the United States to halt plans for cruise missiles and Pershing IIs and upon the Soviet Union to halt the SS-20. It calls for an expanding nuclear-weapons-free zone in Europe, and envisages the gradual loosening of allegiances to either bloc. It calls on individuals, East or West, to act for common survival without regard for the interests or prohibitions of national states. It sets forth a strategy of lateral exchanges across the continent, from Poland to Portugal, and it demands freedom of communication and exchange of information, East and West.

The thrust to final war continues. But we have, at least, generated a small counter-thrust. And what we have discovered is that, even in 'this unhappy day', the process is not finally determined by technology or strategy; there is still a space in which people and opinion can move. Even the media which, a year ago, seemed impermeable to rationality have opened new spaces here and there, revealing in their midst not only SLOBs but also concerned citizens, themselves anxious that democratic discourse should be resumed.

We could have done none of this without the channels of objective information which you among others have helped to hold open. We have now been able to hand on this information to a growing European public. Our strategy is neither against the United States nor against the USSR. If successful, we hope that a nuclear-weapons-free zone in Europe might take some of the sting out of the Cold War's venom, and provide a shield or space between the superpowers in which tensions would lessen. It might help to save both giants from themselves.

NOTES

1. Nigel Calder, *Nuclear Nightmares*, Penguin, October 1981, London.
2. George F. Kennan, 'Politics and the East-West Relationship', *Just for the Press,* III, No. 5, Nov-Dec 1980 (American Committee on East-West Accord).
3. See Louis René Beres, *Apocalypse: Nuclear Catastrophe in World Politics* (Chicago, 1980), pp. 56–57.
4. The classic statement is, of course, President Eisenhower's valedictory address: Eisenhower, D.D., *Public Papers of the President,* 1960–1961, p. 1038.
5. Earl Mountbatten's speech is available (with addresses by Lord Philip Noel-Baker and Lord Zuckerman) in *Apocalypse Now?* (Spokesman Books, Nottingham, U.K., 1980).
6. Lord Zuckerman, 'Science Advisers and Scientific Advisers', *Proceedings of the American Philosophical Society,* 124, No. 4, August 1980. Offprints of this essential text available from the Menard Press, 23 Fitzwarren Gardens, London N19 3TR.
7. See Deborah Shapley, 'Arms Control as a Regulator of Military Technology', *Daedalus,* 109, Winter 1980.
8. Zuckerman, op. cit., p. 13, who also calls on the evidence of H. Scoville, *Missile Madness* (Boston, 1970): 'The guilty men and organizations are to be found at all levels of government and in all segments of society'—and a formidable list of officers, persons and motivations is then given.
9. Zuckerman, op. cit., p. 13.
10. My own most pessimistic conclusions are in 'Notes on Exterminism, the Last Stage of Civilisation', below.
11. See Mary Kaldor, 'Disarmament: the Armament Process in Reverse', in Dan Smith and E.P. Thompson (eds.), *Protest and Survive* (Penguin Books, London, 1980).

12. Calder conjures up 'freedom fighters', p. 64. Beres treats the problem extensively. See also Mason Willrich and Theodore Taylor, *Nuclear Theft: Risks and Safeguards* (Cambridge, Mass., 1974).
13. These are, of course, US intelligence code-names for Soviet missiles.
14. My fuller comments on this episode are in E.P. Thompson, *Writing by Candlelight* (Merlin Press, London, 1979).
15. For an objective account of the techno-strategic and diplomatic sequence surrounding the NATO decision, see Milton Leitenberg, *NATO and WTO Long-Range Theatre Nuclear Forces* (SIPRI).
16. See my 'The Domesday Consensus' in *Writing By Candlelight.*
17. *Defence in the 1980s. Statement on the Defence Estimates,* Cmnd. 7826-1, HMSO, London, April 1980.
18. See Christopher Paine's admirable study, 'Pershing II; the Army's Strategic Weapon', *Bulletin of the Atomic Scientists,* 36, No. 8 (October 1980), esp. p. 30.
19. Robert Havemann, 'After the Thirty Minutes War', in *END Bulletin* No. 3.
20. This perception is shared by Paul C. Warnke: 'If I were a European, the last thing in the world I would want would be to have more theatre nuclear forces, because I would think that would make me all the more certain to be the first target at the beginning of a war': interview in the *Guardian* (London), September 28, 1980.
21. Britain is displaced at the head of the league table by West Germany, because of the stockpiling of all the 'small' stuff there—the 'tactical' or battlefield weapons.

NOTES ON EXTERMINISM, THE LAST STAGE OF CIVILISATION

Comrades, we need a cogent theoretical and class analysis of the present war crisis. Yes. But to structure an analysis in a consecutive rational manner may be, at the same time, to impose a consequential rationality[1] upon the object of analysis. What if the object is *ir*rational? What if events are being willed by no single causative historical logic ('the increasingly aggressive military posture of world imperialism', etc.)—a logic which then may be analysed in terms of origins, intentions or goals, contradictions or conjunctures—but are simply the product of a messy inertia? This inertia may have drifted down to us as a collocation of fragmented forces (political and military formations, ideological imperatives, weapons technologies): or, rather, as two antagonistic collocations of such fragments, interlocked by their oppositions? What we endure in the present is historically-formed, and to that degree subject to rational analysis: but it exists now as a critical mass on the point of irrational detonation. Detonation might be triggered by accident, miscalculation, by the implacable upwards creep of weapons technology, or by a sudden hot flush of ideological passion.[2] If we drill all this in too tidy a logical formation we will be unprepared for the irrationality of the event. Twenty-one years ago, in the forerunner to this journal, Peter Sedgwick (addressing the arguments of a different moment) alerted us to this irrationality:

> A conspiracy theory was implicit in all analysis produced from within the Stalinist orbit. 'The ruling circles of the United States' were 'bending all their efforts to prepare a new war', 'fresh plans of aggression' being constantly prepared by these very circles. A

This article first appeared in *New Left Review*, No. 121, May-June 1980.

criminal foresight was thus ascribed to the enemy, in a manner both implausible and alien to Marxist categories. What Wright Mills calls 'the drift and thrust towards World War Three' is indeed to be ascribed to the existence of oligarchic and military ruling classes (whose distribution over the continents of the globe is, incidentally, somewhat more widespread than the Partisans of Peace ever hinted). But the danger of war arises not from conscious planning on the part of the elites. . . If this were so, we could all sleep safely, for the 'ruling circles' would hardly be likely to plot their own annihilation. . . War is possible as the outcome of policies initiated by these irresponsible minorities, *as the final unforeseen link in a causal chain forged at each stage by the previous choice of some ruling class.* World War Three could burst out as 'something that no one willed'; the resultant of competing configurations of social forces. . . If Man is ever obliterated from the earth by means of his own armaments, there will be no simple answer to the question: Did he fall, or was he pushed?[3]

Twenty-one years on, and the immediacy of this question, as well as the political demands of the moment, break up the mind. I can offer no more than notes, fragments of an argument. Some fragments must take the form of questions, addressed to the immobilism of the Marxist Left.

The Deep Structure of the Cold War

A swift caricature of whatever theory underlies this immobilism would run like this. It is in stance *a priori:* the increasingly-expert literature on weaponry, militarism, and in peace research remains unread.[4] It is informed by a subliminal teleology: history must move through its pre-programmed stages, do what men will, and we may refuse, with religiose optimism, Marx's grimmer option: 'the mutual ruin of the contending classes.' It confuses origins with consequences. And it confides in an anthropomorphic interpretation of political, economic and military formations, to which are attributed intentions and goals. Since the 'cause' of the Cold War is commonly ascribed solely to the evil will of 'imperialism', it then becomes possible to analyse events in terms of imperialism's supposed rationality (however malevolent these reasons) rather than in terms of the irrational outcome of colliding formations and wills.

In its story-line it goes something like this. The original, and also the replicating, cause of Cold War lies in the drives of world imperialism. These drives are then analysed, with attention to Africa, South-East Asia, Latin America, and with a peroration about the Middle East and oil. China is invoked as part of the revolutionary heritage: its inconvenient diplomatic and military postures are then forgotten.[5] Europe is passed over without analysis, except in its accessory role in world imperialism. State socialism, however 'deformed' (and here Marxists of different persuasions offer different grade-marks for deformity), has a military posture which is 'overwhelmingly defensive'. This can be confirmed by an *a priori* exercise, through a brief attention to differing modes of production and social systems: the capitalist mode is motivated by the drive for profit and for new fields of exploitation, whereas the arms race imposes an unwelcome burden upon socialist states (however deformed) by diverting resources from socialist construction.

As for the Bomb, that is a Thing, and a Thing cannot be a historical agent. Preoccupation with the horrors of an imaginary nuclear war is diversionary (did not the Vietcong call that bluff?), and it leads to hideous heresies, such as 'neutralism', 'pacifism', and to utter confusion in the class struggle. CND exemplified such capitulations to moralism and 'pacifism', which is why it 'failed'. Meanwhile, the anti-imperialist struggle prospers in the Third World (Vietnam, Angola, Iran, Nicaragua, Zimbabwe), and eventually it will be carried thence to the 'barbarians' in the capitalist heartlands.[6] The best that these barbarians can do, while they wait, is to engage in frontal class confrontation until the capitalist economies begin to buckle.

But there might be other ways to situate our analysis. We would examine, less origins, than the consequences of consequences. We would attend with care to military technology, strategy and formations. We would confront the possibility of war with a controlled pessimism of the intellect. We would read the immediate past as the irrational outcome of a collision of wills, and we would expect the immediate future to enlarge that irrationality.

I can only glimpse the story-line that this might give us.

But it would, I think, replace Europe, and, at a short remove, China, at the centre of the story. It would start from the US-USSR polarisation, and, by extension, the USSR-China-US triangle. What is known as the 'Cold War' is the central human fracture, the absolute pole of power, the fulcrum upon which power turns, in the world. This is the field-of-force which engenders armies, diplomacies and ideologies, which imposes client relationships upon lesser powers and exports arms and militarisms to the periphery.

On the periphery there is still political mobility, and the story-line already given is acceptable enough, although more distorted (and distorted into militarist forms) by the dull enforcements of the central poles than the story usually allows. In exceptional cases, where the polar antagonism is so acute that conventional military intervention would bring the immediate probability of US-USSR confrontation, the space for political mobility is actually enlarged: Iran and the Middle East are the obvious examples.[7] But along the central fracture, political mobility has been, for thirty years, congealed: at worst, it assumes degenerative forms. And here we must acknowledge not one but two imperial formations, however different their origin and character. For the Soviet Union, which extends from the Baltic States to Mongolia, includes within its strategic imperatives all that inflammable human material in Eastern Europe which must be held perpetually under political, military and ideological controls.

It must become clear already that 'imperialism' is an inadequate category to encompass more than a part of this situation of global contradiction and collision. It is a situation without precedent, and it becomes lost to view when we try to stuff it into inapposite categories. It is a situation both of antagonism and of reciprocity, for the increment of weaponry on both sides takes place in part according to a reciprocal logic, and is even regulated by elaborate agreed rules. The MX missile is a clever device to stretch to the limits without rupturing the games-plan of SALT II: each missile will chunter on tracks between a number of concealed firing-points, but inspection-covers will periodically be thrown open to Soviet satellite observation to reassure 'the enemy' that there is only one missile in each track-system.[8]

In this games-plan it matters less than may be supposed to define the military posture of the Soviet Union (or of 'the West') as 'basically defensive'. That is no more than a moralistic attribution of supposed intention. Both superpowers are mounted and armed for instant annihilating attack. Barbed wire, pillboxes, trenches, anti-tank guns—the accessories of a Maginot Line—might be categorised as 'defensive' weapons, but ICBMs may not.

The Bomb is, after all, something more than an inert Thing. First, it is, in its destructive yield and its programmed trajectory, a thing of menace. Second, it is a component in a weapons-*system*: and producing, manning and supporting that system is a correspondent social system—a distinct organisation of labour, research and operation, with distinctive hierarchies of command, rules of secrecy, prior access to resources and skills, and high levels of policing and discipline: a distinctive organisation of production, which, while militarist in character, employs and is supported by great numbers of civilians (civil servants, scientists, academics) who are subordinated to its discipline and rules.[9]

It means rather little to peer into the entrails of two differing modes of production, searching for auguries as to the future, if we are so inattentive as to overlook what these modes produce. For, increasingly, what is being produced by both the United States and the USSR is the means of war, just as, increasingly, what is being exported, with competitive rivalry, by both powers to the Third World are war materials and attendant militarist systems, infrastructures and technologies.[10]

There is an internal dynamic and reciprocal logic here which requires a new category for its analysis. If 'the hand-mill gives you society with the feudal lord; the steam-mill, society with the industrial capitalist', what are we given by those Satanic mills which are now at work, grinding out the means of human extermination? I have reached this point of thought more than once before, but have turned my head away in despair. Now, when I look at it directly, I know that the category which we need is that of 'exterminism'.

The Logic of Nuclear Weapons Systems

Originism and anthropomorphism have no need to examine weaponry and strategy. Weapons are things, and strategies are instrumental plans for implementing policies which originate elsewhere. Thus what we must do is examine the ruling elites and their political intentions. All the rest can be taken as given.

This sounds like commonsense. But it is wrong. It is to foreclose analysis of self-generating independent variables before it has even commenced. Nuclear weapons (all weapons) are things: yet they, and their attendant support-systems, seem to grow of their own accord, as if possessed by an independent will. Here at least we should reach for that talisman, 'relative autonomy'.

This increment in the means of extermination is, of course, the outcome of someone's choice. But where do such choices originate? Are they political or technological choices? The answer is complex. One part of the answer is that, given the defences of official secrecy–defences almost impermeable in the Soviet Union–we do not know.

The rival arsenals of the USA and USSR stood at 6,500 substantial nuclear weapons in 1960: at 14,200 in 1979: and, even within the games-plan of SALT II, will arrive at some 24,000 *strategic* weapons by 1985.[11] Analysts used to explain this steady, and accelerating, increment according to a simple action-reaction model: 'Implicit in this view were the ideas that the decisions of leaders actually determined force structure and that leaders' orders were carried out by the military bureaucracy. . . It implied that the leaders of each side reacted rationally to the behaviour of the other side. . .'[12]

This rationality is now challenged. Weapons innovation is self-generating. The impulse to 'modernise' and to experiment takes place independently of the ebb and flow of international diplomacy, although it is given an upward thrust by each crisis or by each innovation by 'the enemy'. Weapons research evolves according to long waves of planning, and the weapons for the year 2000 are now at the R & D (research and development) stage. Deborah Shapley defines this incremental pressure as 'technology creep', owing to its 'gradual, inconspicuous, bureaucratic character'.

Its modes differ: US weapons increment is more active and innovative, USSR increment more reactive, imitative, and in the form of 'follow-on' modifications.

But in both powers there is a steady incremental pressure more inexorable than can be explained by recourse to notions of an 'arms lobby' or a military 'interest'. Shapley lists as factors, in the United States, 'the enthusiasm of scientists for advertising the potential of their work, the interest of program managers and design bureaus in testing improvements, and the armed services' wish to have the most up-to-date versions of their systems.' Alva Myrdal adds 'the inter-service competition for shares of the military budgets, leading to an arms race within the arms race'—a competition evident in Britain now as service chiefs compete around the 'successor' to Polaris—and the 'mental virus' of the 'technological imperative'. Zuckerman identifies similar forces: 'the men in the laboratories', the 'alchemists of our times', who 'have succeeded in creating a world with an irrational foundation, on which a new set of political realities has in turn had to be built'. He implies ('working in secret ways which cannot be divulged') that official secrecy prevents him from further revealing their mode of operation and political impingement.[13]

This does not seem a sufficient explanation for a thrust which is absorbing a significant proportion of the world's GNP, and which is manifestly irrational even in military terms (weaponry for adequate mutual 'deterrence', or mutual assured destruction (MAD) already existed, in the absence of any effective anti-ballistic missile defences, some twenty years ago). What Shapley and Zuckerman do not emphasise, and what any socialist would insert into the argument, is the competitive drive of capitalist arms producers, a drive which has become more intense within the shadow of recession. We will return to this important component of exterminism in a moment.

Yet it is not clear to me that we have found a simple explanation for this incremental thrust in profit-taking (in the West) and in action-reaction (in the East). Weapons research, in both blocs, originates in bureaucratic decisions rather than out of the play of market forces. The state is always the customer: and, in market economies, the state guarantees the high—even arbitrary—profit return, which is passed on (often in hidden allocations) to the taxpayer. Arms manufacture may take place in the public or the private 'sector', but even where, as in the United States, there is acute competition between private enterprises for the state's tender, the number of competitors is diminishing, and covert agreements are normal between the great competitors to ensure a 'fair' division of the spoils. We do not need the profit motive to bring us to extermination, although it helps. Ideology and a general bureaucratic inertial thrust help more.

There is no profit motive in the Soviet Union: *ergo,* the 'fault' for the arms race lies only with 'the West'. How do we know this? Can states and bureaucracies not have motives for arming? The briefest survey of historical, as well as contemporary, evidence will tell us that they can. The decisive point for Soviet armament increment appears to date from around the time of the fall of Khrushchev: from the mid-1960s, there has been a steady growth in nuclear weaponry, as well as development and modernisation of the armed forces. In terms of differential growth, the pace of the Soviet armourers seems to accelerate in the 1970s, during the 'quiet' years of detente; by a stupendous concentration of resources and scarce scientific skills, the Soviet armourers reached forward until nuclear weapons 'parity' with the United States seemed within their grasp. At the same time, the Soviet navy was deployed as an active world presence. Similar economic and technological decisions as in 'the West' (economies of scale, long production runs) have underwritten the entry of Soviet armourers as major salesmen in the markets of the Third World. Figures for all these matters are ideologically-contaminated and in dispute: but socialists who refuse them any credence (as figments of CIA propaganda) are sadly ill-informed. The facts are of this order.[14]

Obviously, political decisions influenced this increment. The political elite in the Soviet Union 'decided' to pursue that infinitely-receding objective of nuclear weapons 'parity', and at the same time to signal its world presence as a military and naval power. But then, *how* did the elite arrive at this decision? Under what pressures were its policies and ideology militarised?

Weapons, to be sure, are things. Their increment is not independent of political decisions. But politics itself may be militarised: and decisions about weaponry now impose the political choices of tomorrow. Weapons, it turns out, are political agents also.

Weapons, and weapons-systems, are never politically-neutral. When European settlers with muskets encountered Red Indian tribes with bows and arrows, the politics of the matter were determined by the barrels of their guns. If the settlers had only had bows and arrows, this would have imposed upon them the politics of the peace-pipe and the parley. As to 'the Bomb', the refinement of nuclear weaponry has been steadily eroding the interval in which any 'political' option might be made. The replacement of liquid by solid fuel means that rockets may now stand in their silos, instantly ready. The time of delivery has contracted: in the mid-1970s the time required for the interhemispheric delivery of nuclear bombs had shrunk to about ten minutes, and it is now perhaps less.[15] This hair-trigger situation, combined with the increasing accuracy of missiles and automated electronic reaction-systems, has encouraged fantasies that a war might actually be launched with advantage to the aggressor ('taking out' every one of the enemy's ICBMs in their case-hardened silos), or that a 'limited' war might be fought in which only selected targets were 'taken out'.

In such a hair-trigger situation, the very notion of 'political' options becomes increasingly incredible. The persons who decide will not be a harrassed President or First Secretary (perhaps not available at the moment of emergency) but a small group of military technicians, whose whole training and rationale is that of war, and who can, by no conceivable argument, be said to represent the rational interests of any economic or political formation. Very probably they will act without any 'political' mediation: already, in the Cuban missile crisis, American naval commanders engaged in the exceedingly hazardous tactic of forcing Soviet submarines to surface, in pursuance of standard operating procedures during a red alert and without the knowledge of the US President.

Today's hair-trigger military technology annihilates the

very moment of 'politics'. One exterminist system confronts another, and the act will follow the logic of advantage within the parameters of exterminism.

The 'Theatre' of Apocalypse

In extremity this may be so. But, surely, there is a long political terrain to be travelled first, before we reach an unlikely extremity (from which it is best to avert our eyes)? And surely strategic decisions are no more than the projections upon the global map of prior political choices?

This is wrong again, or half-wrong. Military strategy is not politically non-aligned. NATO 'modernisation' with cruise missiles and Pershing IIs is a case in point.

Strategy imploded upon West European political life at Brussels on 12 December 1979, in a supposedly technological-strategic decision to 'modernise' NATO nuclear armoury. Ground-launched cruise missiles on European territory are the hardware designated by US strategists for a 'limited' or 'theatre' war. They are commended for their extreme accuracy, even if the claims for CEPs (Circular Error Probable) of only a few hundred feet may be empty brags.

They implode upon politics for two reasons. First, they translate the notion of 'theatre' war from fantasy to actuality. ICBMs carry such colossal destructive power that they do, in fact, deter. Even military strategists, while multiplying warheads, can see the irrationality of ICBM warfare. The militarists have unprecedented resources, which, however, they can never put to use. Hence extreme impatience builds up, most notably in the Pentagon, to design some new games-plan, which would advantage the power superior in nuclear technology. In this re-writing, Soviet strategists are unaccountably unco-operative: 'Recent moves in NATO have encouraged plans for selective, discreet strikes rather than all-out exchanges. . . Unfortunately, the Soviet Union has shown little interest in Western ideas on limited nuclear war. . .'[16]

Even so, the Soviet hand might be forced: faced with a *fait accompli*–limited 'theatre' war ('taking out' selected targets in Russia as well as 'taking out' most of Europe) might be imposed upon the Soviet Union if the clear alternative was ICBM obliteration. This would then be a victory for 'the free West'.

The pressure rises upwards from the laboratories and the strategic war-games simulation rooms to NATO planning committees (co-opting on the way the compliant cowboys who inhabit the Institute for Strategic Studies[17] and the Royal Institute of International Affairs) to the United States Secretary of Defense and to the President's national security adviser (the prime architect of the Iranian helicopter fiasco), Zbigniew Brzezinski:

> *Brzezinski:* I think you see already the beginning of a serious review manifesting itself in the Secretary of Defense's defense posture statement, in being able to respond to nuclear threats in a flexible manner, in the serious thought being given to our nuclear targeting plans, in the much higher emphasis being placed on command and control capabilities.
>
> All of these reviews are designed to enhance our ability to bargain in the context of severe crisis, to avoid a situation in which the President would be put under irresistible pressure to preempt, to avoid leaving the United States only the options of yielding or engaging in a spasmodic and apocalyptic nuclear exchange. *Question:* Are you saying that you want the United States to be able to fight a 'limited' nuclear war? *Brzezinski:* I am saying that the United States, in order to maintain effective deterrence has to have choices which give us a wider range of options than either a spasmodic nuclear exchange or a limited conventional war. . .[18]

The only unaccountable element in this whole operation is the fact that NATO politicians have eagerly endorsed a 'choice', by United States strategists, to designate their territories as the 'theatre' of apocalypse. What has happened is that an option of astonishing political dimensions has been imposed upon West Europe in the anodyne vocabulary of strategy and technology. In fact, in this case the strategy was invented long before the weapons. The embodiment of 'flexible-response' strategy was endorsed by NATO as early as 1967; was enforced by Schlesinger; and was a matter of open discussion among experts in the early 1970s. It was in 1975 that the American analyst, Herbert York, wrote with admirable candour: 'Today's Western Europeans have chosen to buy current political stability by placing awful risks. . .

over their lives and their future. Perhaps their choice was inadvertent; perhaps they did not and even today still do not realise what they have done. . .'[19]

US strategy by then had already adopted the imperative that the United States should be a Sanctuary, and that nuclear war should be limited to external 'theatres': West Europe was designated (without the knowledge of its peoples) as the sacrificial proxy. That the peoples of West Europe did not 'know' of this new designation was the effect of official secrecy and the management of information; that intellectuals (and socialist intellectuals) did not know merits less excuse—Herbert York and Alva Myrdal were there for us to read.[20] The new generation of missiles to match this strategy was in advanced development by the mid-1970s. What has been presented in the West European media, and in debates in West European parliaments, in the last few months as a regrettable but necessary 'response' to the Soviet SS-20s was set in motion before the SS-20 had been heard of. It is difficult to know whether these politicians are plain liars, illiterates, or the victims of polluted civil service briefs.

The final act of 'decision' was registered, at Brussels, in a non-elective, quasi-political, quasi-military assembly: NATO. The fantasy was translated into fact in a series of elaborate bureaucratic planning steps, inscribed with runic acronyms: NATO's LTDP (Long-Term Defence Programme), NPG (Nuclear Planning Group), and HLG (High Level Group). From 1977 to 1979 the NPG and HLG scurried through secretive meetings at Los Alamos, Brussels, Fredrikshaven, Colorado Springs, Homestead Air Force Base (Florida), etc.[21] NATO then 'requests' the US government, in its generosity, to send this can of rattlesnakes across to the designated theatre, and, in the same instant, notifies European governments that they are to receive them.

One watches, spellbound, the bureaucratic forms of exterminism. I do not mean that 'strategy' or 'bureaucracy' did all this unaided. No-one could have been more abject in their complicity than Mrs Thatcher and Mr Pym. I mean only to note that a prior condition for the extermination of European peoples is the extermination of open democratic process. And I am inviting readers to admire the style of the thing.

The second reason why this military hardware implodes upon our political life is this. Cruise missiles are, with finality, *committing.* Ground-launched, operated solely by US personnel (whatever evasive parliamentary provisos are made about 'consultation'), they commit this nation absolutely to strategic imperatives imposed by Sanctuary USA. In every crisis, someone else's finger will be upon 'our' trigger.

Cruise missiles are *committing:* strategically, but also politically. They place us, with finality, in the games-plan of the Pentagon. True, F-111s which, during the Iranian helicopter fiasco (and we know what 'consultation' went on then) were placed at Lakenheath on nuclear alert, are committing also. But the cruise missiles have a new kind of political visibility, a manifest symbolism of subjection. That is why they must be repelled.

This is not—need one say this?—to urge a reversion to the old sloganry of 'national independence'—'Yankees Out'! The cause of European Nuclear Disarmament (END) is only one point of engagement in the international struggle for peace. The alert, generous and growing North American peace movements will understand this and will give us their support, just as (in quieter and more complex ways) opinion will bring its own pressures to bear in the Soviet Union also. For no 'theatre' war which reaches the point of nuclear exchanges will ever be contained within its theatre; it will be, at the most, a matter of days before the ICBMs launch off, and Washington and Moscow, Utah and West Siberia, are brought within the 'theatre'. END will provide a shield, just as other shields must be formed in the Pacific and the Middle East.

It is not the 'Yankees' but the exterminists who must be called out—and, first of all, our own. Two vignettes: returning through the US base at Upper Heyford, Oxfordshire, after the march against cruise missiles on 17 May 1980, one loud and over-enthusiastic marcher was shouting abuse at the American personnel: he was promptly taken in custody, by the *British* police. One North American marcher politely engaged in conversation a black American airman who was on his way out of the base. Was it true, she asked, that this was a British base, or was it really an American one? The airman commenced to offer a courteous reply: he was promptly interrupted and taken off in custody, by the *American* military security police.

The Scope of Self-Determination

There is a contradiction in the logic we have traced above. The diplomacy of ICBM annihilation increasingly polarises the world into absolute antagonism. Yet, since the launching of these missiles is the final act, the room for the deployment of the lesser means of war becomes, except at the periphery, increasingly restricted and hazardous. The client states of each grand alliance are reduced to impotence: they surrender their fate into the keeping of the Great Stockpile.

Examine the possible sequence of events in Iran, if the helicopter operation had not providentially aborted. (1) US troops, with miscellaneous CIA auxiliaries, arrive in Teheran. (2) Bloody fighting, the release of a few hostages, and the slaughter of the rest. (3) The USA bombs Iranian installations or mounts a punitive expeditionary force, in revenge for the slaughter of hostages, and to save the Presidential face. (4) The Iranian government appeals to the Soviet Union for military aid. (5) Confrontation. The point is that, at each stage of this sequence, the client states of NATO would have remained wholly captive and without 'consultation'.

It is in the face of such sequences that Britain and France make their pitiful and expensive gestures at maintaining an 'independent deterrent'. Polaris and the French S3 are aimed, not at the Warsaw powers, but at the White House. If they can commit us, we must maintain at least a mini-bluff that we can commit them. Trident will be purchased for £5,000 million or more pounds to buy a modicum of influence upon the Pentagon. As a 'deterrent' against the Soviet Union, Polaris, Trident and S3 are absurd: they are no more than our own pistols, and the right to determine the moment at which we will blow out our own brains.

But within this contradiction, little opportunities sometimes appear. The nations which resume mobility are those which detach themselves from either pole. Non-alignment brings an increment in real diplomatic influence. The superpowers must court stubborn Yugoslavia: captive Britain need not be noticed at all. European Nuclear Disarmament–the expulsion of weapons and bases, and detachment from bloc diplomacies–will be an act of self-determination, striking at the most sensitive points of power.

The Thrust of Exterminism

But that is a utopian vision. Let us return to the deep structure of the Cold War, or the thrust of exterminism.

Figures gesture only at process. Global figures are slippery digits. But by some calculations, the percentage of the world's GNP expended upon armaments has run, at any time since World War II, at between 6 per cent and 8 per cent, whereas in the run-up to the previous two world wars it was never higher than 3 per cent.[22] The current United States and NATO powers commitment to an *annual* increment, in real terms, of 3 per cent plus in arms budgeting (an increment which, no doubt, will be matched by the Warsaw powers, and also by China) may well push this towards 10 per cent in the next few years.

This may not appear as a fearsome figure until we appreciate three things. First, this production is concentrated in the economies of the advanced powers. The 'European-oriented alliances' (NATO and Warsaw powers) were responsible, in the mid-1970s, 'for about four-fifths of the total world military expenditure'.[23] This affects in radical ways the structuring of advanced economies. Second, such figures (derived from declared budgets) give only a partial view, since various support-systems for militarism (scientific, ideological) are civilian in character and their cost is masked.

Finally, this small figure (8 per cent) indicates the allocation of a surplus withdrawn from circulation, services and consumption. It is this surplus which we often take to be indicative of the priorities, the embodied symbols of temporal authority or of spiritual aspiration, which mark the character of a civilisation. That surplus, worked up into artefacts, indicates what holds men and women in thrall and what they worship: the great tumuli, the megalithic circles, the temples, the pyramids, the great medieval cathedrals, the giant rockets in their silos, the MX missile system.

The MX missile project is noble in scope, greatly exceeding

the prospects of any prior civilisation in its grandeur. It will occupy a 6,000-square-miles complex in Nevada and Utah; require 10,000 miles of roadway; the missile-tracks will move, on 200 individual loops, between 4,600 case-hardened shelters. Security extensions and approach roads, with ancillary installations, may increase the total occupied area to 20,000 square miles. It is a greater, and far more expensive, project than the Panama Canal or the Alaskan pipeline system.

Undoubtedly, the MX missile-system will be the greatest single artefact of any civilisation. It will be the ultimate serpentine temple of exterminism. The rockets in their shelters, like giant menhirs pointing to the sky, will perform for 'the free West' not a military but a spiritual function. They will keep evil spirits at bay, and summon worshippers to the phallic rites of money. Within the aura of those gigantic nuclear circles, the high priests of ideology will perform ritual sacrifices of taxes. In distant outposts of the faith, at Westminster, Brussels, and the Hague, Druidical servitors will bow low to the West and incant missilic runes.

Many Millennia afterwards, visiting archaeologists from another planet will dig among the still-radioactive embers and debate the function of the great temple. The debate will be in vain. For the temple will be erected to celebrate the ultimate dysfunction of humanity: self-destruct.*

Nuclear Economics

What both modes of production are now, increasingly, producing are nuclear weapons, tanks, submarines, small arms, nerve gas, etc.[24] Of course, some of this production is consumed: that is the privilege of the Third World, whose military expenditure has increased four-fold in the past two decades: from 10 per cent of the global total in 1960 to 24 per cent in 1978. The rate is accelerating. Over the same period Third World GNP was calculated to increase by a factor of 2.7, but military expenditure by 4.2. The major competitors in the Third World's arms market were, in 1978, the USA (47 per cent), the USSR (27 per cent), France (11 per cent), and Italy and the UK with 4 per cent each.[25] But

* The MX project has now (February 1982) been cut down in size and shifted in site, no doubt in response to my criticisms.

non-aligned Austria and the nation of the Good Soldier Schweik are pushing for their share in the killing.

This is not contingency. It is process. The long waves of the armourers do not move in phase with the waves of diplomatic confrontation. Each international crisis legitimates the process, and strengthens the upswing. But in quiet periods of 'detente' there is an autonomous incremental logic. In the post-war years, the arms race has been like a rocket with three successive stages of thrust: the first Cold War, the Vietnam war, and, then, after a levelling off, the third upward thrust in the mid-1970s, in the midst of 'detente'. The French S3 which came into operation in May 1980 was commenced in 1974. The 'Chevaline' modernisation of the Polaris warhead, at a cost of £1,000 millions, was devised in the early 1970s, authorised by Mr Heath in 1973, bequeathed to Sir Harold Wilson, carried forward secretively by Mr Callaghan, and announced triumphantly to a startled parliament in January, 1980, by Mr Pym. We have seen that current NATO missile 'modernisation' was prepared in the mid-1970s. The upswing in US military expenditure commenced at the same time: US Defence procurement increased from $45.8 billion in 1976 to $55.6 billion in 1977 and $69.0 billion in 1979. The US Defence budget for 1981-5 is projected at $1 trillion. The increment in Soviet armaments appears to have taken off in the late 1960s and to have been more steady, a product of fewer political variables and of central allocations of plan, although certain surges can be attributed to an action-reaction model. Paradoxically, the SALT I agreement (1972), purporting to establish ceilings for numbers of strategic weapons, provides an example. US strategists assented to these clauses in the foreknowledge that they could make nonsense of them by placing several MIRVs (multiple independently-targeted re-entry vehicles) on each missile. In response Soviet armourers successfully developed their own MIRVs by 1975.

It may comfort socialists to see a 'cause' for this primarily in Western imperialism, and only secondarily in Soviet reaction. This is now beside the point. To argue from origins, to nominate goodies or baddies, is to take refuge from reality in moralism. Nations which have been exposed to unremitting destructive attack, famine, and civil war (Cambodia), or which liberate themselves by a prolonged and total sacrificial military self-organisation (Vietnam), do not emerge unchanged, to choose between policy options according to theoretical persuasion or moral intention. Superpowers which have been locked, for thirty years, in the postures of military confrontation increasingly adopt militaristic characteristics in their economies, their polity and their culture. What may have originated in reaction becomes direction. What is justified as rational self-interest by one power or the other becomes, in the collision of the two, irrational. We are confronting an accumulating logic of process.

This logic, while reciprocal, is not identical. In the United States a strong contributory thrust to exterminism comes from the normal dynamics of gigantic capitalist enterprise. Moreover, one can observe a collective capitalist General Will for survival or expansion, whether as counter-revolutionary reaction to indigenous anti-imperialist movements in the Third World[26] or whether in pursuit of interests and resources (notably oil) of the most old-fashioned imperialist kind.

Emma Rothschild, in a cogent journalistic essay, has recently re-stated (and up-dated) the argument that in the post-war decades the military industries have functioned in the United States, just as cotton did in the industrial revolution in Britain, as the 'leading sector': not 'as a single or multiple industrial sector. . . but rather as a cluster of industries joined by a common objective and a common customer.' Given an expanding market, and an assured, high, rate of profit, this leading sector has in turn stimulated the boom in electronics, civil aerospace, etc., as well as in secure enclaves of civilian research and development. She suggests that it is this leading sector which has both paced the long wave of growth and determined the national economic structure, in conformity with Schumpeter's criteria of 'breaking up old and creating new positions of power, civilisations, valuations, beliefs and policies'.[27]

Rothschild argues also that this boom is entering upon cyclical decline. It is a sector which carries its own contradictions. It generates both inflationary pressures and unemployment, since the manufacture of advanced weaponry is capital-intensive. It has its own forms of technological obsolescence, as innovation becomes harder to achieve.[28]

But a business boom on the edge of a bust is a snarling, irrational beast. It might even appear that as American hegemony faltered, in the aftermath of Vietnam defeat, and as arms expenditure levelled off, efforts to re-invigorate the leading sector became more deliberate, more highly-conscious, and more highly ideological and political in character.[29] What had been 'unconscious' process began to become, when threatened, conscious of itself: impulsive exterminism began to grow an exterminist mind and will. The immense security operations, the organs of political manipulation and information control, revealed by Watergate were not the product of Nixon: they were the natural civilian and ideological support-system for the military-industrial complex. Nixon's blunders exposed them to view, but they have long been resurgent.

Now, in 1980, crisis arrives–Afghanistan, Iran–and is eagerly welcomed. Ageing, overweight arms industries re-collect the vigours of their youth. Huge injections of public money are brought to their rejuvenation. 'Defence Stocks Lead Market Up' is the response of the *Wall Street Journal* to Brown's latest budget. Lobbyists (who are often former Pentagon personnel hired by arms contractors) descend on the Pentagon: McDonnell Douglas, Boeing, General Dynamics, Grumman, Lockheed, General Electric, Westinghouse, Chrysler, ATT. Congressmen are approached with promises of investment in their districts. Bribes and excessive commissions oil the procedures. Lobbying extends to regional and local military and air force units, and also to the Defence ministries and assemblies of NATO powers. The regular chime of contracts is announced, like the gazetting of top appointments, in the press. A random example–

> Lockheed Missiles & Space Co. unit received an $18.2 million Navy contract for engineering service for ballistic missiles.
>
> Grumman Aerospace Corp. was awarded an $8.7 million Air Force contract for horizontal tail stabilizers for F-111 fighter bombers.
>
> GK Technologies Inc. said its Automation Industries Inc. subsidiary

has received a $9.6 million contract from the Navy for research, development, test and evaluation of weapons systems. . .

Southland Oil Co. got a $4.2 million contract from the Defense Logistics Agency for jet fuel. . .[30]

The MX missile system is not yet put to contract. In June 1979 it was costed at $33 billion. By early 1980 it was costed at $56 billion. By mid-April of 1980 estimates had risen to over $100 billion.[31] The best plum to be landed so far in 1980 has been the $4 billion deal for 3,418 cruise missiles for the US air force. Although Boeing is the winner, some part of the killing will, by quiet pre-agreement, be divided with its rivals.[32]

I cannot, as is well known, understand economics. I leave all this to more competent minds to evaluate. But somewhere within these matters lies one part of the thrust towards extermination.

The Inertial Push of Soviet Policy

We look in vain for comparable thrusts within the placid, plannified features of Soviet bureaucracy. Indeed, if one is not a specialist in Soviet affairs, one looks in vain for anything (NATO propaganda apart), since the press opens up few inspection-covers, and no Watergate scandal affords us a momentary glimpse of the exterminists about their humdrum daily chores of power.

In trying to envisage the nature of Soviet process, I find an analogy with an ill-run, security-conscious university with a huge and overmighty engineering department, so powerful that it can nominate the Vice-Chancellor and the Registrar, dominate the Senate, nobble most of the research funds, attract all the gifted graduates, and pack every committee. The engineering department is of course the military-industrial 'interest'. We are examining, not the self-production and invasive properties of capital, but the self-production and imperative pressures of a bureaucracy.

The Soviet state was born in military struggle: consolidated a ramshackle empire into a Union by military struggle.

In the 1930s the priority upon heavy industry had a heavy military accent: militarism was built, not only into the superstructure, but into the base. And militarism inevitably found a huge (and popular) extension in the Great Patriotic War. In a significant sense, the Soviet has always been a 'war economy'.[33]

Arms-related industries have always received the first priority for scarce resources, including skilled manpower; the good conditions of work and pay attract 'the most highly skilled cadres'. In 1970, when arms expenditure had levelled off, in the United States one-quarter of all physicists, one-fifth of all mathematicians and engineers, were engaged in arms-related employment.[34] Today's proportions are probably higher. No comparable figures can be cited for the USSR, but there are strong grounds for supposing that, in a less highly developed economy which has, by a remarkable concentration of resources, developed its weapons-systems close to the point of parity with the United States in force and in sophistication, a significantly higher proportion of the nation's most skilled physicists, engineers, chemists, mathematicians, experts in electronics and cybernetics, are concentrated in this sector.

The arms complex is as clearly the leading sector of Soviet industry as it is in the United States, but this is expressed within bureaucratic modes of operation. There is some spin-off from military technology into civilian industry: civil aircraft, nuclear energy. But Soviet weapons technology, which is paced by its sophisticated American competitor, has opened up a gap between itself and its civilian compatriots: 'recent military technology has become too sophisticated for. . . cooperation to be possible'.[35] The military complex and its successes are upheld as a model of organisation and of management techniques, and these are exported to other sectors. Moreover, the needs of the military complex—in particular, the imperatives placed upon centralised planning, priority in access to resources, and direction of scientific skills—affect the structure of the economy as a whole, and colour the decisions of the political managers. It is the threat which might be afforded to the stability and interests of this complex which inhibit any introduction of 'market' mechanisms into the economy as a whole.[36]

At the same time there is a greater direct exposure of the Soviet population to patriotic state propaganda than in most Western democracies: that is, what is (or is attempted to be) accomplished in 'the West' by the 'free' operation of the media is directly inculcated in Russia by such 'voluntary' organisations as DOSAAF: the Voluntary Society for Co-operation with the Army, Aviation and the Navy, with a membership of 80 millions, and with clubs, sports facilities, and military-patriotic or civil defence education organised around factories, farms and schools. And alongside and supporting all this there are the huge, quasi-autonomous operations of the Security Services, inheriting historic traditions of despotism, supporting military-patriotic ideology, and exerting an independent inertia of their own.

In David Holloway's view, such military-patriotic manifestations are now 'a pervasive feature of Soviet life'.[37] 'The Armed Forces and the defence industry occupy an entrenched position in the Party-state apparatus. The high priority which the Party leadership has given to military power has thus become institutionalised.'

But while military officers are awarded high status and privilege, and their influence can be seen at the highest level of political life, that influence (as in 1953, 1955 and 1964) has not been decisive. The interest has been mediated by the Party, and it would be mistaken to view the military–*yet*– as an autonomous interest. Brezhnev, who emerged with close experience of the military-industrial sector and with its backing, has satisfied its aspirations.

In this view, the incremental thrust in the Soviet Union towards extermination is not aggressive and invasive, but is ideological and bureaucratic. Yet it has, in Holloway's view, acquired an autonomous inertia, embedded in the structure of Soviet society, and can no longer be ascribed to reaction in the face of Western exterminism:

> Foreign influences are refracted through the Soviet policy-making process, in which Soviet perceptions, military doctrine, foreign policy objectives and domestic influences and constraints come into play. The effect of foreign actions on Soviet policy is complex

> and not at all automatic. In many cases the foreign influences combine with domestic factors to speed up the internal dynamic of Soviet arms policies. The very existence of large armed forces, a powerful defence industry and an extensive network of military R & D establishments generates internal pressures for weapons development and production. . . As a system progresses from conception to development, military and design bureau interests become attached to it, building up pressure for production. If it passes into production. . . enterprise managers are likely to favour long production runs.

It does not look, under this analysis, like an aggressive thrust. Yet it is a dangerous inertial push, with its own hawkish imperatives of ideology and strategy (Czechoslovakia, 1968: Afghanistan, 1980), and which could afford nourishment to a popular culture of chauvinism, xenophobia, and even (when confronting China) racism. It is the more dangerous in that it is unchallenged by democratic exposure: no-one may ask, in public, why–after the first ICBMs were in place–the absurd yet decisive decision to match each weapon and to attain to 'parity' was ever taken? Only for a brief period, under the impetuous and contradictory Khrushchev, does an erratic challenge appear to have been offered to the process, and this challenge was offered by the First Secretary himself: a distinct fall-back in the rate of weapons increment, an explosive speech about 'the metal-eaters', even (as in generous non-military aid to the Third World[38] and as in the long personal exchanges between Russell and Khrushchev) a glimpse of an alternative, internationalist strategy, summoning up a non-aligned movement for peace.

Thereafter inertia assumed the helm: ideological paranoia, fear of dissent, the null orthodoxy of official Soviet intellectual life, terror at Eastern European deviation, hostility at authentic non-alignment or even at Eurocommunist autonomy–all this going along with the games-play of top persons 'detente',[39] with SALT this and SALT that, with increasingly-military injections of 'aid' to the Third World, and with the emplacement of the foul and totally unnecessary SS-20 on Europe's margins: a weapon which beckoned on, like a cue in the common script of exterminism, the entry of NATO's waiting cruise missile. The Soviet inertial thrust may be as humdrum as the cooked minutes of a captive Senate, but when in collision with the hectic thrust of capital, it will do for us all.

Annihilation and Security

Let us attempt to assemble these fragments.

I am offering, in full seriousness, the category of 'exterminism'. By 'exterminism' I do not indicate an intention or criminal foresight in the prime actors. And I certainly do not claim to have discovered a new 'exterminist' mode of production. Exterminism designates these characteristics of a society—expressed, in differing degrees, within its economy, its polity and its ideology—which thrust it in a direction whose outcome must be the extermination of multitudes. The outcome will be extermination, but this will not happen accidentally (even if the final trigger is 'accidental') but as the direct consequence of prior acts of policy, of the accumulation and perfection of the means of extermination, and of the structuring of whole societies so that these are directed towards that end. Exterminism requires, of course, at least *two* agents for its consummation, which are brought into collision. But such collision cannot be ascribed to accident if it has long been foreseen, and if both agents have, by deliberate policy, directed themselves upon an accelerating collision-course. As Wright Mills told us long ago, 'the immediate cause of World War III is the preparation of it'.[40]

The clearest analogies are with militarism or imperialism (of whose characteristics exterminism partakes). These may be found to characterise societies with different modes of production: they are something less than social formations, and something a good deal more than cultural or ideological attributes. They designate something of the character of a society: of its drive: and the direction of that drive. Militarism and imperialism are founded upon actual institutional bases (the military, the navy, the chartered trading companies and slavers, the arms manufacturers, etc.), from which they extend influence into other areas of life. In mature forms they appear as whole configurations (institutional, political, economic, ideological), and each portion reflects and reinforces the other. Exterminism is a configuration of this order, whose institutional base is the weapons-system, and the entire economic, scientific, political and ideological support-system to that weapons-system—the social system which researches it, 'chooses' it, produces it, polices it, justifies it, and maintains it in being.

Imperialism helps us both by analogy, and also by revealing the point at which analogy breaks down. Imperialism normally predicates an active agent and a subjected victim: an exploiter and an exploited. Vulgar imperialist theory tended to become enmeshed in an argument from origins: the drive for markets, raw materials, new fields for exploitation—if the originating 'motive' could be identified, this was held to explain all. Yet this failed to explain, not only many episodes—strategic and ideological imperatives, the expectation of rewards, the reciprocal influence of the subjected upon the imperial power—but also the irrationality (in terms of the pursuit of self-interest) of climactic imperial moments: in imperial rivalries, in the First World War, in fiercely-irrational ideologies which contributed to Fascism. It becomes necessary, then, to see Western imperialism as a force which originated in a rational institutional and economic matrix, but which, at a certain point, assumed an autonomous self-generating thrust in its own right, which can no longer be reduced by analysis to the pursuit of rational interests—which indeed acted so irrationally as to threaten the very empires of its origin and to pull them down.

So far, the analogy is helpful. This gives us the character of exterminism in the 1980s. No doubt we will have one day a comprehensive analysis of the origins of the Cold War, in which the motives of the agents appear as rational. But that Cold War passed, long ago, into a self-generating condition of Cold War-ism (exterminism), in which the originating drives, reactions and intentions are still at play, but within a general inertial condition: which condition (but I am now asking a question which will, I hope, be refuted) is becoming irreversible as a direction.

This is not because of the irrationality of political leaders (although this often helps). It is because the inertial thrust towards war (or collision) arises from bases deeply enstructured within the opposed powers. We tend to evade this conclusion by employing concepts which de-limit the problem: we speak (as I have done) of the 'military-industrial complex', or of the military 'sector' or 'interest' or the arms 'lobby'. This suggests that the evil is confined in a known and limited place: it may threaten to push forward, but it can be restrained: contamination does not extend through the whole societal body.

But the more apposite concept, which is employed by some peace researchers,[41] is that of isomorphism: 'the property of crystallising in the same or closely related forms', or 'identity of form and of operations as between two or more groups'. Viewed in this way, the USA and the USSR do not *have* military-industrial complexes: they *are* such complexes. The 'leading sector' (weapons-systems and their supports) does not occupy a vast societal space, and official secrecy encourages low visibility; but it stamps its priorities on the society as a whole. It also inflects the direction of growth. In the US 1981 budget $16.5 billion is allocated to 'research, development, test and evaluation' (RDTE) of weaponry. Of this less than 10 per cent (a mere $1.5 billion) is allocated to MX research. But–'This is more than the combined RD budgets for the Department of Labor, the Department of Education, the Department of Transportation, the Environmental Protection Agency, the Federal Drug Administration, and the Center for Disease Control; over 140 per cent of the RD budget of the National Science Foundation.'[42] Given the technology gap between the two powers, and yet the extraordinary sophistication of Soviet weaponry, the inflection of the direction of Soviet research must be even greater.

Science-intensive weapons-systems civilianise the military: but in the same moment more and more civilians are militarised. The diplomacy of 'posture' and bluff, together with the drive to steal some technological advantage, generate covert intelligence operations and the policing of information. The need to impose assent on the public (the US taxpayer, the Soviet consumer whose rising expectations remain unsatisfied) generates new resources to manage opinion. At a certain point, the ruling groups come to *need* perpetual war crisis, to legitimate their rule, their privileges and their priorities; to silence dissent; to exercise social discipline; and to divert attention from the manifest irrationality of the operation. They have become so habituated to this mode that they know no other way to govern.

Isomorphic replication is evident at every level: in cultural, political, but, above all, in ideological life. In a notable letter addressed last year to the California Board of Regents, Gregory Bateson, the social scientist, employed an analogy from biological systems:

> The short-time deterrent effect is achieved at the expense of long-time cumulative change. The actions which today postpone disaster result in an increase in strength on *both* sides of the competitive system to ensure a greater instability and greater destruction if and when the explosion occurs. It is this fact of cumulative change from one act of threat to the next that gives the system the quality of *addiction.*

Frustrated aggression 'backs up' until it permeates whole cultures.

It is within ideology that *addiction* to exterminism is distilled. The confrontation of the superpowers has, from its origin, always had the highest ideological content: ideology, as much as profit-making and bureaucratic growth, has motored the increment of weaponry, indicated the collision-course, and even (on occasion) sheltered some victims.[43] In both camps ideology performs a triple function: that of motivating war-preparations, of legitimating the privileged status of the armourers, and of policing internal dissent. Over more than thirty years, anti-Communism has been the means of ideological control over the American working class and intelligentsia; over the same period Communist orthodoxy has imposed ideological controls by a simple 'Stalinist' reversal.

The two camps are united ideologically in only one matter: in mutual hostility to any genuine non-alignment, 'neutralism', or 'third way'. For if such a way were to be possible, it would strike directly at exterminism's legitimacy. Dubcek and Allende must be overthrown, because they have trespassed upon the most sensitive territory of ideology: their success would have challenged the very premises of the mutual ideological field-of-force. The contagion might have spread, not only through Eastern Europe and Latin America, but to the heartlands of exterminism themselves.

The concept of isomorphism provides a clue to developments in the past decade in Britain. In this client state of NATO with its faltering economy, crystallisation proceeds with unusual rapidity: Official Secrets trials, burgeoning security and surveillance, the management of Official Information and of 'consensual' ideology, the positive vetting of civil servants, the rising profile of the police, jury vetting, the demotion of parliamentary and other democratic process, the oiling of the machinery of 'national emergency', the contingency planning of the Cabinet Office, the futilities of *Protect and Survive.* While industries wither on the vine, and while 'public expenditure' is hacked at with a Friedmanite axe, new weapons-systems are planned and public money is flushed down the exterminist sluice.

Britain, as it enters the 1980s, offers itself as a caricature of an exterminist formation. The imperatives of 'defence' poison the nation's economy; the imperatives of ideology deflect even profitable weapons-manufacture into the hands of United States contractors. The subordinate inertial thrust of the national weapons-system-complex augments the imposts of NATO: a motive for the £1,000 million 'Chevaline' programme, we learn, was 'finding something for the large scientific establishment at Aldermaston. . . to do'.[44] The politicians who initiated these weapons-systems have now left the scene; their successors are now no more than a reflexive part of the support-system for these systems,[45] along with the civil servants, the scientists, the Treasury officials, the television controllers and the defence correspondents who afford these systems logistic supply and protection.

Even here where I write, in the rural West Midlands, I can sense the presence of neighbours: at Cheltenham, the headquarters of the GCHQ signals interception: at Hereford, the base of the SAS: at Kidderminster, the manufacture of propellant for 'Sea-Slug' missiles (which came to public notice only after fatalities in an explosion): at Malvern, research into radar, but also into officially-secret things.

It is a cumulative process, crystallisation in culture accelerating crystallisation in the economy, and thence to politics, and thence back again once more. Security operations impinge upon politicians; job security in weapons industries impinges upon trade unions; expansion in military research, usually in the 'public sector', generates bureaucratic pressures in Britain much the same as the bureaucratic thrust of the Soviet managers; the Minister of Defence and the Foreign Secretary carry in their portfolios (to China, Oman, Pakistan) the briefs of arms salesmen; and at home, academics are funded to prepare these briefs. Since all these pressures accumulate in the direction of extermination, it is proper to designate them as exterminist.

The Moment of Greatest Danger

The analogy with imperialism takes us a long way, but in the end it breaks down. Imperialism calls into being its own antagonist in the movement for self-determination of the people of the subjected country. Exterminism does not. Exterminism simply confronts itself. It does not exploit a victim: it confronts an equal. With each effort to dominate the other, it calls into being an equivalent counter-force. It is a non-dialectical contradiction, a state of absolute antagonism, in which both powers grow through confrontation, and which can only be resolved by mutual extermination.

Yet exterminism does generate its own internal contradictions. In the West, a science-intensive war economy produces not only weapons-systems but inflation, unemployment, and deteriorating services. In the East, a war economy slows down and distorts the direction of growth, and generates shortages of resources and skills. The strains are felt most acutely in the client states of both alliances, where resentment grows against their captive state. As anxiety and dissatisfaction mount, there can be glimpsed, as an intolerable threat to exterminist ideology, the possibility of a truly internationalist movement against the armourers of both blocs.

This brings us closer to the point of crisis. An accelerating thrust has set the superpowers upon collision course, and the collision is to be expected within the next two decades.[46]

Yet the economies and ideologies of either side could buckle under this acceleration. The injections of public money, even the MX missile, may not stave off US recession: it might even aggravate its form, in the disjunction between an advancing and a recessive economy.[47] In the Soviet Union and in Eastern Europe it is ideological crisis which is most manifest: how long will those old controls work? The official description of reality induces only tedium; ideology is no longer internalised–it becomes a mask or a patter learned by rote, whose enforcement is a matter for the police.

As we know from history, this conjuncture of crisis and opportunity is the most dangerous moment of all. The ruling groups, habituated to the old modes and controls, sense the ground moving beneath them. The hawks and doves form factions. Actions are precipitate and impulsive. Neutralism, internationalism–democratic impulses in the East, socialist impulses in the West–appear as hideous threats to established power, challenging the very *raison d'être* of exterminist elites. In that situation of impending superpower collision and of ideological instability, it is not likely that 'we'–with our poor resources, our slight political preparation, our wholly inadequate internationalist communications–can succeed. It is probable that exterminism will reach its historical destination.

The Direction of Hell

I have been reading *Arguments within English Marxism,* and, leaving aside local disagreements and assents, have been puzzling over an ulterior difference of stance which neither I nor Perry Anderson have exactly defined. Which difference I will try to identify, in response to Anderson's invitation 'to explore new problems together'–even though this problem is an old one. It is, absurdly, one of generational experience.

My generation were witnesses, and petty actors, in the actual moment of the congealment of the Cold War, and the fracture of power across Europe. That fracture (enlarging the fracture of the 1920s and 1930s) has always seemed to me to be the locus of the field-of-force whose polar antagonisms generate exterminism.

The second generation of the New Left, who have

conducted its *Review* so long and so tenaciously, arrived on the scene when the Cold War had already congealed, and its ideological imperative had become a habit. At some point around 1960, Khrushchev's erratic pursuit of detente together (I would argue)[48] with the growth of CND-type peace movements in the West had offered a check to the exterminist thrust, had forced it to disguise its operations and to modify its aggressive vocabulary. Nuclear war (it was agreed on all sides) was 'unthinkable'.

But at the same time, on the periphery (and South-East Asia was then still on the periphery) a new mobility of national liberation and revolutionary movements was in evidence, which met with a savage Western response. The new generation of the Left was quick to identify this whole opening field of struggle: expert in attention to it: and eloquent in theoretical solidarity with anti-imperialist movements in Africa, Asia and Latin America.

In all this they were right. But in the same moment preoccupation faded with the central emplacements of power: and it came to seem (wrongly) that confrontation between the two blocs *originated* at the periphery, and was carried only thence *to* the centre, so that its thrust and dynamics could be simply explained within the categories of imperialist thrust and anti-imperialist resistance. The role of western socialists became, more and more, to be that of observers and analysts of that external confrontation.

To my generation, which had witnessed the first annunciation of exterminist technology at Hiroshima, its perfection in the hydrogen bomb, and the inconceivably-absolute ideological fracture of the first Cold War (the Rajk and Rosenberg trials, the Cominform anathema upon Yugoslavia, McCarthyism and the advocacy of 'preventive war', the Berlin air-lift and the Berlin wall), this never seemed so. We had become, at a deep place in our consciousness, habituated to the expectation that the very continuation of civilisation was problematic.

This expectation did not arise instantaneously with the mushroom cloud over Nagasaki. But I can, in my own case, document it fairly exactly. In 1950 I wrote a long poem, 'The Place Called Choice', which turned upon this expectation. The central section of the poem concluded thus:

> . . . Spawn of that fungus settling on every city,
> On the walls, the cathedrals, climbing the keening smoke-stacks,
> Drifting on every sill, waiting there to germinate:
> To hollow our house as white as an abstract skull.
>
> Already the windows are shut, the children hailed indoors.
> We wait together in the unnatural darkness
> While that god forms outside in the shape of a mushroom
> With vast blood-wrinkled spoor on the windswept snow.
>
> And now it leans over us, misting the panes with its breath,
> Sucking our house back into vacuous matter,
> Helmeted and beaked, clashing its great scales,
> Claws scratching on the slates, looking in with bleak stone eyes.

Such an apocalyptic expectation, which has never left me, is no doubt discreditable. Hans Magnus Enzensberger, whom I much respect, has recently chided the futurologists of doom, the 'negative utopians'; 'the world has certainly not come to an end. . . and so far no conclusive proof has reached me that that an event of this kind is going to take place at any clearly ascertainable point in time'.[49] And, of course, it would be worse, far worse, than an apocalypse for one to make oneself intellectually ridiculous. I would only too gladly read the arguments which show, conclusively, that my analysis of the gathering determinism of exterminist process is wrong.

Yet the arguments have substance, and the technology of the apocalypse exists. Nor have all apocalyptic visions in this century always been wrong. Few of those who prophesied World War I prophesied the devastating sum of the actual event; no-one envisaged the full ferocity of World War II. And the apocalyptic prophets of World War III do not match the kind of persons we encounter in our social history: eccentric vicars, zealous artisan sectarians conning *Revelation,* trance-struck serving-maids. Some emerge, with strategic war-plans in their hands, from the weapons-system complex itself: Sakharov, Mountbatten, Admiral la Rocque,

Zuckerman. It was not Joanna Southcott who summoned the first Pugwash Conference, but Einstein and Russell. It was not Thomas Tany but Robert Oppenheimer who said, in 1947, 'the world is moving in the direction of hell with a high velocity, a positive acceleration and probably a positive rate of change of acceleration'.

We should, even in the matter of apocalypse, be a little exact. An exterminist climax might be aborted by a 'limited' local nuclear war (China, Africa, the Persian Gulf) whose consequences were so terrible that these frightened even the exterminists, and called up a new global wave of resistance. And even outright exterminist collision, with the full repertoire of ICBMs in the northern hemisphere would not necessarily extinguish all mammalian life, unless the globe's ozone layer was irreparably punctured.

What this would destroy would be northern civilisation and its economic and societal life-support systems. The survivors (one might suppose) would then be exposed to waves of plague and famine; great cities would be abandoned to rats and to rattish genetic mutants. People would scatter to un-contaminated lands, attempting to re-invent a sparse economy of subsistence, carrying with them a heavy inheritance of genetic damage. There would be banditry: fortified farmsteads, fortified monasteries, fortified communes; and a proliferation of strange cults. Eventually there might be the re-emergence of petty city states, nudging towards new trade and new wars. Or this scenario could be all wrong. Advanced economies might survive, relatively undamaged, in the southern hemisphere: Australia, Argentine, South Africa. After an interval for stench and plague to die down, these might come back, with their muskets, to colonise the European tribes: perhaps to fight over the spoils: perhaps to establish one superpower's world dominion.

I do not mean the extermination of all life. I mean only the extermination of our civilisation. A balance-sheet of the last two millenia would be drawn, in every field of endeavour and of culture, and a minus sign be placed before each total.

Our Opportunity

If one has come to live with this expectation, then it must

modify, in profound and subtle ways, one's whole political stance. Class struggle continues, in many forms, across the globe. But exterminism itself is not a 'class issue': it is a human issue. Certain kinds of 'revolutionary' posturing and rhetoric, which inflame exterminist ideology and which carry divisions into the necessary alliances of human resistance, are luxuries which we can do without.

There are contradictions within this gathering determinism, and countervailing forces in both blocs, as to which I have said, in these notes, very little. It remains to indicate what an anti-extermininist configuration of forces might look like, and what its strategy might be, if it were to stand any hope of success.

First, it would have to mobilise itself with great rapidity, since we are already within the shadow of collision. Prophecies are arbitrary: but the successful emplacement of cruise missiles on West European territories in 1983 might signal a point-of-no-return.

Second, the fracture through the heart of Europe remains the central locus of the opposed exterminist thrusts, although the second fracture in Asia (with the unpredictable presence of China) is growing in significance.[50] Hence European Nuclear Disarmament is not a strategy for opting out of global confrontation. It strikes directly at that confrontation, by initiating a counter-thrust, a logic of process leading towards the dissolution of both blocs, the demystification of exterminism's ideological mythology, and thence permitting nations in both Eastern and Western Europe to resume autonomy and political mobility. Neutralism or non-alignment in any part of the globe are not, or are not necessarily, isolationist or 'pacifist' options: they are active interventions against exterminism's determinist pressures.

Third, this configuration must, as a matter of course, forge alliances with existing, anti-imperialist and national liberation movements in every part of the world. At the same time, by strengthening the politics of non-alignment, it will develop a counter-force to the increasing militarisation, in Africa and Asia, of post-revolutionary regimes.

Fourth–and this may be the most critical and decisive point–it must engage in delicate and non-provocative work to form alliances between the peace movement in the West and constructive elements in the Communist world (in the Soviet Union and East Europe) which confront the exterminist structures and ideology of their own nations.

This is of necessity; and without such internationalist alliances which reach across the fracture we will not succeed. The exterminist thrust (we have seen) summons up and augments the thrust of its exterminist antagonist. The counter-thrust can not come from the other, but only from within the resistance of peoples *inside each bloc.* But so long as this resistance is confined within its own bloc, it may inhibit the thrust of war but cannot finally impose alternative directions. So long as each bloc's resistance movement can be categorised as the 'ally' of the other, exterminism (with its powerful bases in the weapons-systems-and-support-complex) will be able to police its own territory, reassert ideological control, and, eventually, resume its thrust.

Hence only the regeneration of internationalism can possibly summon up a force sufficient to the need. This internationalism must be consciously anti-exterminist: it must confront the ideological imperatives of both blocs: it must embody, in its thought, in its exchanges, in its gestures, and in its symbolic expressions, the imperatives of human ecological survival. Such a movement cannot be mediated by official or quasi-official spokespersons of either bloc. (This fact was signalled by those Euro-communist parties which refused their attendance at the Paris conference in April 1980.) The strategy of Stockholm Peace Appeals and of the World Peace Council is as dead as is the strategy (prizing open Soviet civil rights by means of US Senate resolutions) of the exile at Gorky.

Internationalism today demands unequivocal rejection of the ideology of both blocs. The rising movement in Western Europe against NATO 'modernisation' must exact a real price from the Soviet ideologists and military managers, in the opening of Eastern Europe to genuine exchanges and to participation in the common internationalist discourse. This must not be a hidden tactic but an open and principled strategy. This may be a most critical point in the dissolution of the exterminist field-of-force. It will be contested with equal ferocity by the ideologists of NATO and by the Communist bureaucracy and police. It will require symbolic manifestations and a stubborn internationalist morale. And it will bring friends into danger.

Finally, it should go without saying that exterminism can only be confronted by the broadest possible popular alliance: that is, by every affirmative resource in our culture. Secondary differences must be subordinated to the human ecological imperative. The immobilism sometimes found on the Marxist Left is founded on a great error: that theoretical rigour, or throwing oneself into a 'revolutionary' posture, is the end of politics. The end of politics is to act, and to act *with effect.* Those voices which pipe, in shrill tones of militancy, that 'the Bomb' (which they have not looked behind) is 'a class question'; that we must get back to the dramas of confrontation and spurn the contamination of Christians, neutralists, pacifists and other class enemies–these voices are only a falsetto descant in the choir of exterminism. Only an alliance which takes in churches, Eurocommunists, Labourists, East European dissidents (and not only 'dissidents'), Soviet citizens unmediated by Party structures, trade unionists, ecologists–only this can possibly muster the force and the internationalist elan to throw the cruise missiles and the SS-20s back.

Give us victory in this, and the world begins to move once more. Begin to break down that field-of-force, and the thirty-year-old impediments to European political mobility (East, South and West) begin to give way. Nothing will follow on easily and as a matter of course: but swing those blocs off collision-course, and the blocs themselves will begin to change. The armourers and the police will begin to lose their authority, the ideologists will lose their lines. A new space for politics will open up.

Within the threatening shadow of exterminist crisis, European consciousness is alerted, and a moment of opportunity appears. These notes are rough, and readers will wish to amend them. I ask them also to act.

1. I am using 'rationality' in these notes to denote the rational pursuit of self-interest, as attributed to a nation, class, political elite, etc. In a different perspective none of these pursuits may appear as rational.
2. I take the British adventure at Suez (1956), the Soviet intervention in Czechoslovakia (1968), and the United States helicopter operation in Iran (1980) to be examples of such hot flushes. The Soviet intervention in Afghanistan is a military-political act of a more calculated order: perhaps a cold flush.
3. Peter Sedgwick, 'NATO, the Bomb and Socialism', *Universities & Left Review*, 7 Autumn 1959. (My italics.)
4. The literature is now extensive. For a preliminary evaluative bibliography, Ulrich Albrecht, Asbjorn Eide, Mary Kaldor *et al.*, *A Short Research Guide on Arms and Armed Forces*, London, 1978. Also the select bibliography appended to Asbjorn Eide and Marek Thee (eds.), *Problems of Contemporary Militarism*, London 1980. Bibliographies are regularly updated in the ADIU *Report* (Science Policy Research Unit, University of Sussex).
5. And will, I fear, be forgotten through most of these notes. I find Chinese diplomacy inscrutable.
6. See Régis Debray, 'A Modest Contribution to the Rites and Ceremonies of the Tenth Anniversary', NLR 115, May-June 1979.
7. At any time before the 1960s, the exactions of OPEC or the truculence of Iranian students would have very certainly elicited a Western military punishment.
8. Herbert Scoville, Jr, 'America's Greatest Construction', *New York Review of Books*, 20 March 1980.
9. Mary Kaldor, 'The Significance of Military Technology', in *Problems of Contemporary Militarism*, pp. 226–9.
10. See M. Kaldor and A. Eide (eds.), *The World Military Order. The Impact of Military Technology on the Third World* (1979).
11. I take here the conservative estimates of Deborah Shapley. These do not include lesser weapons. In other counts, if all nuclear weapons are included, the world's sum has already passed 50,000.
12. Deborah Shapley, 'Arms Control as a Regulator of Military Technology', *Daedalus*, 109, Winter 1980.
13. Alva Myrdal, *The Game of Disarmament*, New York 1976, pp. 11–12; Lord Zuckerman, 'The Deterrent Illusion', *The Times*, 21 January 1980 (now reprinted in *Apocalypse Now*, Spokesman Books).
14. For a reliable evaluation of the increment in both blocs, see Dan Smith, *The Defence of the Realm in the 1980s*, London 1980, esp. chapters 3 and 4.
15. Alva Myrdal, *op. cit.*, p. 8.
16. Lawrence Freedman, Head of Policy Studies, Royal Institute ofInternational Affairs, in *The Times*, 26 March 1980.
17. 'The threat of a Soviet nuclear attack on Western Europe could leave NATO the choice only of an early resort to the American arsenal, putting American cities at risk. . . Missiles in Western Europe would give the American President an intermediate option': Gregory Treverton, Assistant Director, Institute for Strategic Studies, in *The Observer*, 19 November 1979.
18. Interview in the *New York Sunday Times*, 30 March 1980.
19. Herbert F. York, 'The Nuclear "Balance of Terror" in Europe', *Ambio*, 4, nos. 5-6, 1976.
20. Alva Myrdal, *op. cit.*, chapter two gives a thorough presentation of the whole 'theatre' strategy, published in 1976.
21. A chatty account of this bureaucratic delinquency is given by Stephen R. Hanmer, Jr, in NATO *Review*, February 1980.
22. Stockholm International Peace Research Institute estimates are summarised by Frank Barnaby, 'Global Militarisation', *Proceedings of the Medical Association for the Prevention of War*, March 1980.
23. Myrdal, *op. cit.*, p. 4. But the Third World is catching up, expending in

1978 (Barnaby, *passim*) 24 per cent of the world's total.

24. An illuminating account of the present state of chemical warfare preparedness is in the *Scientific American,* April 1980.
25. Barnaby, *op. cit.*
26. The remarkable survey of the 'American Gulag archipelago' by Noam Chomsky and Edward Herman, *The Washington Connection and Third World Fascism,* and *After the Cataclysm* (both Spokesman Books, 1979) has received less discussion in Britain than it merits, perhaps because of differing interpretations of events in Indo-China. Some of the most terrible episodes (which merit—as do events in Cambodia—the description of exterminist) have been effected by indirection and proxy: see A. Kohen and J. Taylor, *An Act of Genocide: Indonesia's Invasion of East Timor,* TAPOL, 8a Treport Street, SW1.
27. Emma Rothschild, 'Boom and Bust', *New York Review of Books,* 3 April 1980.
28. Since writing this article I have read the important report, 'The Role of Military Technology in Industrial Development', presented by Mary Kaldor to the UN Group of Government Experts on the Relationship of Disarmament and Development, May 1980. Kaldor argues a related but more complex case, with greater emphasis upon 'baroque' military technology: increasingly expensive, sophisticated, ineffectual, and leading to technological distortions or dead-ends. Kaldor sees the weapons-systems industries in the USA and Britain less as a 'leading sector' than as a sector constricting and distorting industrial change, and leading to 'technological stagnation, the symptom of a vicious circle in which industrial decline stimulates military spending which then paradoxically accentuates the process of decline.' She finds the export of such technology to the Third World to be wholly negative, implanting decadence within the very pursuit of growth.
29. See James Petras and Robert Rhodes, 'The Reconsolidation of US Hegemony', NLR 97, and the ensuing discussion in NLR 101–2.
30. *Wall Street Journal,* 4 April 1980.
31. Herbert Scoville, *op. cit.; New York Times* (science supplement), 15 April 1980; *Guardian,* 13, March 1980.
32. *Time Magazine,* 7 April 1980; *Guardian,* 27 March 1980; and, on the activities of arms lobbyists, *New York Times,* 30 March 1980.
33. Oskar Lange, *Papers in Economics and Sociology,* Oxford 1970, p. 102.
34. Rothschild, *op. cit.*
35. Zhores Medvedev, 'Russia under Brezhnev', NLR 117, Sept-Oct 1979, p. 18.
36. Alec Nove, 'Problems and Prospects of the Soviet Economy', NLR 119, Jan-Feb 1980, pp. 16–17.
37. David Holloway, 'War, Militarism and the Soviet State', *Alternatives,* June 1980. See also the same author's 'Soviet Military R & D' in J. Thomas and U. Kruse-Vacienne (eds.), *Soviet Science and Technology,* Washington DC, 1977. I draw heavily upon David Holloway's paper in this section, and thank him for permission to do so, but he is not to be held responsible for my conclusions.
38. See Zhores Medvedev, *op. cit.,* pp. 11–12.
39. See my 'Detente and Dissent', in Ken Coates (ed.), *Detente and Socialist Democracy: a discussion with Roy Medvedev,* Spokesman Books, 1975.
40. C. Wright Mills, *The Causes of World War III,* New York 1958, p. 47.
41. See Jan Oberg, 'The New International Military Order', in *Problems of Contemporary Militarism,* esp. pp. 54–64.
42. Emma Rothschild, *op. cit.*
43. The high ideological visibility of Yugoslavia and of Cuba may have protected them from military operations more than considerations of strategic sensitivity. Contrast the pitiful quasi-official cowboy expedition against Cuba (the Bay of Pigs) with the unprecedented military violence visited upon Vietnam.
44. *Guardian* defence correspondent, 27 May 1980.

45. See the ineffable William Rodgers, then Labour's Defence spokesman in the *Labour Weekly*, 23 May 1980: 'Some three-quarters of a million men and women serve in the forces today or are involved as civilians in support activities and the defence industries. . . If the Labour Party ceased to care about defence, we should lose their support and never win an election again.'
46. If China places herself finally in either bloc, throwing her mass into the scales, it is difficult to see how collision will not occur.
47. See Emma Rothschild, *op. cit.,* and Mary Kaldor, 'The Role of Military Technology in Industrial Development', *op. cit.*
48. I dissent sharply from the analysis offered by Anderson and others which tend to demote CND (pacifist, neutralist, middle-class, 'failed') and to canonise VSC. But, for the moment, this argument can be left aside.
49. 'Two Notes on the End of the World', NLR 110, July-August 1978.
50. By 'locus' I do not mean that Europe is the most probable flash-point for detonation. Pakistan or the Gulf States might provide that.

HUMAN RIGHTS AND DISARMAMENT

Prague, December 12 1980

Dear Edward Thompson

I have learnt about your visit to Prague this year, and of the unexpected course which it took for you. I am convinced of your sincere desire to cooperate with citizens concerned in civic activities in our country, and so I have decided to explain to you the reasons for the reaction which you met with here.

I was pleased by your wish to read the arguments which show, conclusively, that your analysis (which is the ground of your expectations for cooperation with some similar movement in our country) is wrong ('Notes on Exterminism', p. 41). Your analysis as to 'the gathering determinism of exterminist process' assumed an identity in the involvement of both superpowers in the 'exterminist' process which you try to prove. I cannot accept this, nor the direction of your argument, and I shall try to explain my reasons.

You view the interrelation of both the superpowers as it is manifested in their armaments as:

> a situation both of antagonism and of reciprocity, for the increment of weaponry on both sides takes place in part according to a reciprocal logic and is even regulated by elaborate agreed rules.

But it is then by no means unimportant that, despite this, you consider the Soviet superpower somewhat partially. You

A reduced version of this exchange of letters appeared in *New Statesman*, 24 April 1981.

draw the conclusion that 'the incremental thrust in the Soviet Union is not aggressive and invasive, but is ideological and bureaucratic' (*Ibid.* p. 62) and 'overwhelmingly defensive' (*Ibid.* p. 43). But you don't concern yourself with any complex analysis of possible connections between ideology and bureaucracy on the one hand, and aggression with invasion on the other. As a consequence you can then call the undeniable facts of aggression and invasion merely 'dangerous inertial push, with its own hawkish imperatives of ideology and strategy' (*Ibid.* p. 63). But a true analysis of such interconnections in totalitarian regimes shows that the relation between ideology and bureaucracy and aggression and invasion is a necessary one. The source of these necessary interrelations is exterminism based on ideology and terror: that is, ideology is something other than the mere performance of the triple functions you mentioned (*Ibid.* p. 67).

I need not demonstrate this analysis to you, since it is very easily accessible. I refer to Hannah Arendt's *The Origins of Totalitarianism.* Despite some modifications of the Eastern bloc's totalitarianism and of the (still reversible) abstention from the physical mass extermination of populations, since the death of Stalin—as Arendt concedes and explains in the preface to the last edition of *Origins*—it often comes (as in Czechoslovakia, East Germany, Roumania, Vietnam and Cuba) to *the general intensification of ideological extermination by the use of power at all possible levels.* In the words of Václav Havel, now in prison, this means the daily, quiet and inconspicious humiliation of millions. If I may elucidate to you the situation as it is seen 'on the other side' I can say that it is the realisation of Orwell's *1984,* except that the domination of this system, whose principle is the liquidation of human rights, is not world-wide.

This 'except', however, is a very important reality, which essentially restrains the totalitarian system from tightening the screw, and this directly concerns the preconditions for your public activity. For the social system in the Eastern bloc operates as totalitarian, and is essentially different from the system you are living in and criticise. I don't think that you shouldn't criticise it. But I am convinced that the fact of your public criticism of the British political system, and of your public activity in support of that criticism–as, for example, your statement that at the present time 'conservatives of all parties. . . have got us half-way. . . into a managed society, whose managing director is money and whose production manager is the police' (*Writing by Candlelight*, London 1980, p. 211)–is in itself clear proof of the democratic British system, no matter how odd this may sound to you. For there is proof here that, in spite of the expanding bias of the executive branch of government and its influence on the judicial and legislative branches, there still exists the political reality of public opinion to be respected.

Your identification of both blocs according to the principle of 'exterminism' is unacceptable, and it spells a very dangerous naivety which is, unfortunately, not exceptional in the West. Your CND peace-movement, which founds itself on this theoretical naivety, seems therefore to be an unconscious analogy to the short-sighted policy of appeasement in the late thirties. You may consider such an analogy to be unacceptable and unjust, but as a historian you probably know the truth often occurs behind our backs. . .

If you imagine that some peace movement similar to CND should arise in the East it is, from your own preconditions, a consequential naivety whose plain impossibility was stressed by Roy Medvedev. But in Poland there does exist a real nonconformist mass movement. Yet it is, characteristically, not a disarmament movement but a movement defending and promoting human rights: that is, promoting those principles whose suppression is the precondition for the existence of a totalitarian system.

Any disarmament movement is meaningful and hopeful only in the sense of the realisation of its objectives as a human rights movement. Your notion of an opposite method which should be accomplished by 'a logic of process leading towards the dissolution of both blocs, the demystification of exterminism's ideological mythology, and thence permitting nations in both Eastern and Western Europe to resume autonomy and political mobility' (*Notes on Exterminism*, p. 74) are very similar to a mechanical notion of detente. This notion means, in the first place, arms limitation and economic cooperation, and its supporters on the Eastern side intend, and promote, mainly the economic aspects. But some spokesmen in the West expect that military and economic detente will naturally cause detente around issues of human and civil rights. The starting-point of such conception is, as cause and effect, the notion that the increasing rate of armament is the cause for the suppression of human rights. Such cases may be possible in Western democracies, but the situation in totalitarian systems is the opposite. Here the precondition of the system, that is, the suppression of human rights, manifests itself *also* in the increase of armaments, *also* in militarism. If you see this situation inverted then it is a short-circuit, or an optical illusion, by which you judge your own situation to explain a totalitarian system. If you then, in consequence, affirm that it is sufficient to:

> swing those blocs off collision-course, and the blocs themselves will begin to change. The armourers and the police will begin to lose their authority, the ideologists will lose their lines. A new space for politics will open up. (*Ibid.* p. 76).

then it is clear proof of your 'slight political preparation' (*Ibid.* p. 70), but in a different sense than you supposed.

I understand that an increasing number of citizens in Western democracies are made anxious by watching the present growth in armaments, which directly affects their countries and their situation in a possible conflict. Yet if the movement for disarmament commences and operates with such assumptions as are expressed in your own theoretical writings, then it becomes, in consequence, a very influential force which works unconsciously in the interest of a totalitarian system whose aim is world domination based on the liquidation of human rights.

As Neville Chamberlain exclaimed, after Hitler's breach of the Munich treaty: 'I have been deceived!' This was a manifestation of sheer dismay expressed by a man who was seeking for peace; but his political naivety contributed substantially to the rise of World War II. In his *Eighteenth Brumaire of Louis Bonaparte* Marx wrote that history never repeats itself, but when it does so it is always as farce. In the case of Munich, which was by definition a farce, it would obviously be such a farce squared. I would be sincerely glad if such an event does not take place, and if no peace movement should play any role in it.

I think that the core of your conception is to be found in a political assumption which divides political forces into right and left wings. In this framework you concede only a division between conservatives and reactionaries and their opposites: that is, the one defines the other. Yet because of the determining character of totalitarian tendencies, movements and ruling systems in the contemporary world, this division has, I believe, become anachronistic. This dangerous anachronism is due to the fact that the determining line of division seems to lie between totalitarian and democratic streams both at the left and right side of the political spectrum.

I cannot expect that, after reading over this open letter, you will classify me as a voice of 'constructive elements in the Communist world' (*Ibid.* p. 75). But I would like to share the perspectives which you present in your 'Notes on Exterminism', and I have tried to explain my reasons.

The purpose of my letter is to try to explain to you the silence you met with in Prague. If my, perhaps unpleasant, but sincerely-intended words should contribute to a critical revision of your premises for the Campaign for Nuclear Disarmament, then it would spell the first step to possible cooperation.

Yours sincerely,

Václav Racek.

Worcester, 29 March 1981

Dear Václav Racek,

Thank you for writing. I am glad that this discussion has commenced. But it has commenced in the midst of many misunderstandings.

First–and a trivial matter–when my wife and I visited Prague last summer we met with great courtesy and nothing occurred that was unexpected. I am sure that you will understand if I do not enter into details.

I will add only that we are both historians, that the treatment of certain historians in Czechoslovakia is a matter of scandal, and that we wished (if possible) to talk with fellow members of our profession, and (if not) to establish certain facts about their treatment.

In May 1974 a distinguished historical journal with which I am associated, *Past and Present*—a journal which normally does not comment on contemporary events—took the unprecedented step of publishing a protest at the treatment of fellow historians in your country. This declared that, subsequent to 1968, many historians had been deprived of their teaching and research posts; some were unemployed; this one was a taxi-driver, another was a lorry-driver, another a boilerman, in conditions where they had no facilities to pursue their research. The statement concluded: 'We believe that such government oppression of teachers and scholars, with the consequent impoverishment of intellectual life, is reprehensible in any society and should be publicly exposed.'

No doubt this issue of *Past and Present* did not find its way to libraries in Prague, but (like so much other material) went astray in the post. It was hoped that the protest might be of a little service, in view of the fact that several British Marxist historians with an international reputation (Mr Christopher Hill, Professor Rodney Hilton, Professor E.J. Hobsbawm and others) had been associated with the journal from its origin. This hope was disappointed. You will not be surprised to learn that my wife and I formed the opinion, last summer, that the situation had changed very little; and in some ways had changed for the worse.

It is true that on our visit we had hoped to be able to talk with Czech friends about other matters also: about the militarisation of our continent, and about common strategies to meet this. And we did have courteous and informative exchanges on this as well. But several doors were closed to us which we had hoped might have been open.

This gave us disappointment but it gave us no offence. Our support for civil and intellectual rights is unconditional. It is not conditional upon your support for causes which we favour; nor do we support the rights only of those persons who hold certain approved positions. Nor are we quite as insensitive as you may suppose. It is no business of stray Western visitors to go pushing into places where they are not wanted, nor (perhaps) to bring upon their friends the attention of the security services.

And then, again, the business of the movement for European Nuclear Disarmament has to be an open business. It is not a conspiracy. People will come to support it in their own way, in their own time. They cannot be conscripted. First of all, confidence must be built and misrecognitions must fall away.

So let us move on to more important misunderstandings. Your letter assumes that there must be some contradiction between the cause of peace and the cause of liberty, and you clearly suspect that those who work for the first cannot be in earnest about the second. You even suppose that you have to persuade me that the social system you live under is 'essentially different' from my own, and you say that it may sound 'odd' to me to learn that my public criticism of the British political system is itself a proof of the continuing reality of our democratic process.

And why should I have to be persuaded of these things? I have written about them myself, again and again. Much of my work as a historian has involved me in the examination of the sources, the realities, and the limits of our democratic process. It is because this process is now threatened, under the pressure of militarisation, that I write so sharply today.

And why should the defence of British liberties disqualify me in the eyes of Czech libertarians? Do you want liberty only for Czechs? Or only for those in Communist countries? Are there no other threats to liberty, no other kinds of 'totalitarian' regime?

One is forced to ask these hard questions by some recent statements from Russian and East European 'oppositionists'. You tell me that I have an 'inverted view' of situations. No doubt this is true: for both of us, experience is partial. I am equally astonished by the inversions in some East European vision.

I have spoken in East Europe with courageous men and

women, whose persistent integrity in their daily tense confrontation with a brutal security service humbled me; and yet they had constructed in their minds a wholly illusory view of 'the other world', made up from 'Radio Free Europe' and from a habit (indeed, a dogma) of believing always the opposite of whatever official Communist propaganda stated to be so.

I have been told–to give one example–that Allende was a 'Communist dictator', overthrown by a popular general strike. This is not true. Allende was a democratically-elected President, with reformist policies, who was first 'de-stabilised' and then murdered in a military coup. The appalling tyranny, executions, tortures, and purging of all intellectual life in Chile in the years which followed this coup out-rival anything to be seen in Eastern Europe in the past decade.

I do not say this to apologise for, or to excuse, any exercise of arbitrary (and alien) power in your own country. Why should I do so? Why should you? I intend only to illustrate this point: 'Radio Free Europe' does not always tell the whole truth, and *Rude Pravo* is not always lying, even though its authors, by the use of hollow moralistic jargon, do their very best to make it seem so.

The blame for these 'inversions' lies with the propagandists who have lied so often that they have made a lie of the whole world. No doubt the reports of less partial observers, like Amnesty International, do not reach you. They go astray in the post. If they should get through you will find a picture more complex than that of the 'free world' here and a 'totalitarian' (i.e. Communist) world there.

I will argue, further, that you, of necessity, have the more inverted and more partial view of the world. Illness, in individuals, is not always conducive to objective views of the affairs of others: suffering can induce self-preoccupation. It is the same with the illness of nations. I take your nation to be ill, and, indeed, in a state little different from that of an oppressive occupation. How can you be other than self-preoccupied with your own national humiliations and injuries? But the first casualty of such a condition is internationalism.

It is not easy for me to make this criticism. I know that the words which you cite of Václav Havel are true, and I salute him in his prison. Over here we face no risks and suffer only minor discomforts. What right do we have, in the midst of our resources, to argue with you at all?

We have no such right. But, yet, we still have the duty, as intellectual communicators, to explain the truth as we understand it. If we have, through no virtue of our own, more open sources of information and more freedom of expression, then it is our duty to put these to use. Intellectual freedom has a precarious survival on this planet: where it survives it brings with it international responsibilities. If we discern new dangers, it is our duty to warn.

Let us turn, then, to the central matter of your letter. You commence your discussion with a serious misunderstanding: indeed, with a direct misquotation.

You attribute to me the view that Soviet militarism is 'overwhelmingly defensive'. In fact I used these words, within quotation-marks, in the course of three pages of polemical critique of exactly this proposition. Perhaps this error has arisen as a result of mistranslation? How, otherwise, was it possible for you to misread my meaning so, unless you *wished* to do so, and 'knew already' anything which I might wish to argue?

I have argued, on the contrary, that there is no such thing as a 'defensive' nuclear weapon. These are weapons of menace, targeted for attack, capable of inflicting mass extermination; however accurately they are targeted, they will inflict hideous 'collateral' damage. As I wrote in those same pages, the notion that nuclear weapons can be 'basically defensive' (whether for West or East) 'is no more than a moralistic attribution of supposed intention. Both superpowers are mounted and armed for instant annihilating attack.'

Nuclear weapons may be justified within a theory of 'deterrence', but this is not the same as self-defence. And they are so justified, in almost identical terms, by the military and political spokesmen of both blocs. Both blocs talk in terms of military 'balance', of matching each others' weaponry at every level (but every level is higher with every passing year), and (in their saner moments) of 'arms control' which is, however, nothing to do with disarmament but concerns only the reciprocal regulation of the never-ending upwards thrust.

In one sense this is a futile exercise, since sufficient weaponry exists already to destroy both East and West Europe, utterly and beyond recovery, thirty times over. One might suppose that, for effective 'deterrence', once would have been enough. In another sense it is (like so much in political history) a contest for 'face', an exercise in symbolism. The 'language' of this symbolism–the threat to exterminate our human neighbours–is the most barbarous known since the birth of civilisation.

But this is not symbolism *only*. This language is made up of actual weapons, which, with each passing year, become more hideous, more accurate, more refined. And what we, in the peace movement of Western Europe, have been signalling to you urgently is that we may be coming to a point of no return. The opposed blocs are set on a collision-course, and we may be close, already, to that terminus. What commenced as a 'rational' contest of rival national interests is now acquiring its own inertia and irrational dimensions. New factors have entered this situation, and, in particular, two.

First (and this was the theme of my 'Notes') militarisation has entered deeply into the structures of both opposed societies. The research and development of new weapons proceeds according to its own logic, and independently of the supposed occasions in political and ideological conflict. It is not only that skills and resources are diverted to the weapons-system-complex (and its attendant security and policing); this complex becomes, in its turn, the source of strategic, political and ideological forces. I did not argue for the identity of these forces, which find differing bases and expressions in Communist state bureaucracy and in Western 'free enterprise' (whose customer remains the state), but for the *reciprocal logic* of this 'exterminist' process.

Second, for both political and technical reasons (the increasing accuracy of new weaponry), the old theory of 'deterrence'–which was MAD or 'Mutual Assured Destruction'–is now wearing threadbare, and new strategies are visible in which nuclear war is becoming 'thinkable', and is even being rehearsed at the planning stage. Such strategies, which have long been canvassed in the Pentagon, include the notions of 'counterforce' and of 'limited' or 'theatre' nuclear war.

Europe (East and West together) is the most probable of all such 'theatres'. NATO rehearsed such a war in its WINTEX exercises of 1977. In response to a supposed scenario of attack upon Western Germany by Soviet 'conventional' forces, General Alexander Haig signed the order for a limited nuclear first strike upon airfields and supply-lines in East Germany, Poland, Czechoslovakia, Hungary, Roumania and Bulgaria. It was then supposed that the Russians called off their conventional attack, and an armistice was agreed; although many military advisers have warned that it is more probable that *any* nuclear attack will lead on, swiftly, to total nuclear exchange.

The point is that it is politically and strategically acceptable to some United States advisers to consider (and even to make plans and weaponry for) a 'theatre' war in Europe, which they suppose that the USA might 'win' with little damage on its own continent–and that such advisers are now clustered around President Reagan and his new administration.

I find that you, and many other Eastern European defenders of human rights do not even wish to enter a discussion of these matters, although they are very fully documented in expert sources. You swiftly close off any discussion–indeed, any attention to the evidence–by accusing us of 'appeasement' and by throwing suspicion upon our motives. I find the first argument to be mistaken; the second I must confess to find unpleasant.

You propose a very simple, binary view of the world: there is Communist 'totalitarianism' here and the 'free West' there; and allegiance to one or the other must entail assent to the military strategies of either bloc. Why is this? Are there no other possibilities? Has history ever been as tidy as that?

You rest your case upon Hannah Arendt's *The Origins of Totalitarianism,* to which you attribute an absolute, biblical authority. It is your *Das Kapital.* I have long become bored with such doctrinaire absolutisms, whether 'Marxist' or 'anti-Marxist', which refuse all entry to the dialogue with evidence. (I would send you my *The Poverty of Theory,* if I did not know that it would go astray in the post). You refuse to discuss the manifest evidence of the militarisation of our continent today because (some twenty years ago) Hannah Arendt wrote a book which did not discuss it.

Yes, I would like to discuss the strength and limitations of Arendt's views, in a seminar in London or across a cafe table in Prague. That is one of the things (I hope) that we may both work for together. And I would argue with you two things. First, the 'idea' of Communism is more contradictory than you suggest: it holds in tension both 'totalitarian' and democratic elements. The Prague Spring, as well as certain Eurocommunist tendencies today (as in Italy and Spain) testify to the democratic elements.

Second, I would argue, as a historian, that even the best of philosophers oversimplify the historical event. You hang the whole of Communist history, like a line of washing, upon the clothes-line of ideology. But, however influential ideas may be, these are diverted in actuality by a multitude of other events in material and cultural life, all of which, taken together, compose the historical event.

Your notion of the Communist idea (or ideology) is singularly pure: a malevolent ill-will, decisively committed to the suppression of all human rights, the author of militarism and of ideological extermination, and driven towards 'world domination'. It is not difficult to understand why a Czech intellectual may think in this way.

But, even in this case of Czechoslovakia, one wonders if the explanation is not overly theoretic? In such accounts as I have read of the repression of the Prague Spring (for example, Mlynar's *Night Frost in Prague*), the operative motives of the Soviet military and of Warsaw Pact political bureaucrats appear to have had a more pragmatic character. They were concerned, as in the 'Brezhnev doctrine', to maintain, for reasons of strategic *realpolitik,* a ring of client states around the Soviet borders: to hold, at all costs, the gains of World War II.

No doubt a gloss was put upon this action in the rhetoric of solidarity with 'fraternal socialist peoples' and the world-wide cause of Communism. But this rhetoric may mean little, and may be a less effective motive than you suppose. In Czechoslovakia, as in Afghanistan, it took a poor second place to pragmatic strategic and political considerations, considerations which turned upon the contest between the two blocs (with the fear of a Chinese-US military alliance as a further factor).

It is, once again, a reciprocal and reactive process, in which there are always at least two agents, and it cannot be explained by recourse to the simple working out of a malevolent ideology. And I think you have fallen into another, more serious, over-logical assumption.

You assume that because the Western world is more free that *therefore* it must be more peaceful, and that its statesmen must act only with defensive intent. This is a deceptive *non-sequitur,* which can be disproved by the briefest attention to history. Some of the earliest experiments in democracy arose within the heart of empires: the Athenian federation, Republican Rome. As a British citizen I am entitled to remind you of an example nearer in time. Nineteenth-century Britain saw very remarkable extensions of the suffrage, and assertions of liberties of press, speech, belief, organisation, and trade union rights. It was a nice country to live in, most of all for intellectuals, and exiles from continental tyrannies chose it by preference. It was in the British Museum (you will remember) that one of these exiles researched *Das Kapital.* But Britain throughout that century was an expansionist empire, consolidating its power in India and South-East Asia, and taking nearly a half-share in Africa.

A prosperous empire may possibly be able to 'afford', in its metropolis, a little more space for liberty and dissent amongst its own citizens. I do not discount the significance of these internal freedoms, or dismiss them as 'phoney': they were ardently fought for, stubbornly maintained, and remain exemplary for us today. It was even possible for British citizens to mount protests against their own nation's endless little imperial wars; and while these protests were with little effect, they did something (as in India) to inhibit repression and exploitation, and to regularise a rule of imperial law.

My point is only that imperialism, or militarism, can perfectly well cohabit with democracy: indeed, very happily. It may very well be nicer for a critical Czech or Russian intellectual to live in Western Europe or the USA. The conditions for independent intellectual work may be more favourable in most ways. I can very well suppose that this is so. And I am wholly committed to those liberties and rights. But this tells us *nothing whatsoever* about military, or even imperial, dispositions. The question of warlike or peaceful propensities is *another question altogether,* requiring attention to different evidence and a different mode of analysis.

We, in the Western peace movement, are trying to get through to you today, and to warn you about the consequences of this elementary error. The West, and United States militarism in particular, is not, in our considered view, adopting defensive dispositions. This is not so in El Salvador, nor in relation to the Persian Gulf, nor in the menacing decision to introduce cruise missiles and Pershing IIs–forward-based strategic missiles, owned and operated by US personnel, onto European territory.

I do not mean that 'ruling circles' in the United States have a calculated plan to attack the Soviet Union, or to provoke a 'theatre war' in Europe, in league with 'West German revanchism'–or whatever story is leading in *Rude Pravo* now. What is happening is less dramatic, but more serious, than that. There is an immense ideological pressure (supported by the powerful arms lobby) to re-assert American hegemony, after the humiliations in Vietnam and Iran; to achieve American superiority in all fields of weaponry; to impose a military definition of reality, extending into diplomatic and cultural relations; and to reduce lesser nations, including NATO allies, to a status of cliency.

United States postures are provocative and menacing, and Soviet rulers are right to find them so. This is not to say that Soviet militarism is 'only defensive'. Soviet militarism exists in its own right, with its own 'hawkish imperatives'. These do not (I think) include any insane plan to drive, with massive conventional forces, upon the West. I think you may agree that those thousands of tanks (which are the phobia of

Western defence 'experts') are held in readiness for service in places rather closer to you than the Channel ports.

It is to say that both superpowers are locked into a reciprocal contest, in a game which they play according to the same rules (the matching of weaponry, the search for strategic advantage)—a game whose outcome must be the massacre of both parties. It is no longer a question of taking sides, of saying which party is most to blame: it is the game itself which must be brought to an end.

In saying this, I hope that I am reporting not only my own view but the dominant view of the Western peace movement. Of course, we have differences of emphasis. But may I quote here a passage of my own, written not for you, but for discussion among my own people?

> If you press me for my own view, then I would hazard that the Russian state is now the most dangerous in relation to its own people and to the people of its client states. The rulers of Russia are police-minded and security-minded people, imprisoned within their own ideology, accustomed to meet argument with repression and tanks. But the basic postures of the Soviet Union seem to be, still, to be those of siege and aggressive defence; and even the brutal and botching intervention in Afghanistan appears to have followed upon sensitivity as to United States and Chinese strategies.
>
> The United States seems to be the more dangerous and provocative in its general military and diplomatic strategies, which press around the Soviet Union with menacing bases. It is in Washington, rather than in Moscow, that scenarios are dreamed up for 'theatre' wars; and it is in America that the alchemists of superkill, the clever technologists of 'advantage' and ultimate weapons, press forward the politics of tomorrow.
>
> But we need not ground our actions on a 'preference' for one or the other bloc. This is unrealistic and could be divisive. What is relevant is the logic of process common to both, reinforcing the ugliest features of each others' societies, and locking both together in each other's nuclear arms in the same degenerative drift.

In the past year I have spoken to many thousands of people at meetings in Britain and the United States, and have conducted a correspondence reaching to many parts of Europe, and I have found, not total agreement, but a very general assent to this description. And then (the discussion continues) how are the people of Europe, East as well as West, over whose heads this threatening game of the superpowers goes on, to develop some common action—a common strategy to thrust those giants apart?

You reject this common strategy. You prefer to fall back upon a received stereotype of what a peace movement must be, and you condemn the movement for European Nuclear Disarmament unheard. You accuse us of 'appeasement'.

This is a painful accusation, for many reasons.

It brings painful recollections to me, of the end of childhood, when, as a boy of 14, I first became politically aware. It was the time of 'Munich'. My family were anti-fascists, and campaigned against the Munich betrayal, my father interrupting from the floor, with an impassioned speech, a meeting in Oxford summoned to congratulate Sir Neville Chamberlain. There was a notable by-election fought in Oxford in that year, between the Master of Balliol, Mr A.D. Lindsay (a 'popular front' candidate) and a young supporter of Chamberlain (and of 'Munich'), who became notorious for his displays of bad manners, called Mr Quintin Hogg.

Mr Hogg was elected, pupated, and eventually spread glorious wings as Lord Hailsham. As Lord Chancellor of England he is now an eminent member of Mrs Thatcher's government.

The line from Munich to the present day is, then, very direct, but it is not exactly the line you suppose. Nor am I certain that it is agreed, as a matter of historical record, that Neville Chamberlain is sufficiently explained as a naive seeker after peace who was deceived. Other historians have suggested that Chamberlain hoped rather to divert the aggressive Nazi drive from the West, and point it in the direction of the East. Prague was to be a half-way-house to Moscow. This explanation would at least remove from Mr Hogg any accusation of inconsistency.

Your accusation also is painful because my own generation, which was not responsible for Munich, did a little to remedy the matter in the next few years. Many of my contemporaries died in the course of putting right that error. I hope that you will have the candour to allow that the European Left was not absent from that costly restitution.

I recollect these two matters because I wish to remind you that there has been *a tradition* of solidarity between our peoples in the face of tyranny, and a tradition in which the Left has had a presence. You should not turn your back upon this.

Your accusation is painful, also, because *this* accusation, and from a Czech, is what will delight our opponents most. The fact that it is made, by a 'dissident', in *Prague,* must prove the matter, once and for all, without further need for argument. You have thrown that card upon the table—but do you know what man (or missile) means to make the trick?

It is painful, finally, because of the form in which it is made. Our movement for disarmament (you say) is 'a very influential force which works unconsciously in the interests of a totalitarian system whose aim is world domination based on the liquidation of human rights'. Nothing could be plainer, nor prettier, than that. Whatever we say, or think, or argue, that is what we really are.

Finis. But. . . wait a minute! Who taught you to argue in that pretty way? Cannot you recall, nearer to home, critics of your own reality who became, in official statements, 'certain elements who', whatever their intentions, were 'unconsciously' aiding Western imperialism. . . and then were 'objectively counter-revolutionary'. . . and, finally, were 'unmasked' as counter-revolutionary agents?

I do not like this form of argument. It is part of the sick lie of our world, in which whoever is not unambiguously of one 'camp' is 'unconsciously' or 'objectively' of the other, and in which everything, from lyrics to treatises to gestures, is traded into the coinage of the Cold War. It is time that we argued in better faith: received and responded to each others' experience: and took each others' coinage of argument as true.

The movement for European Nuclear Disarmament offers to appease no-one and to forgive nothing. It offers to contest the militarisation of both blocs. In refusing Europe as a theatre of war, it proposes—and I will agree that this may appear as an utopian proposition—to resist in the only way possible: to make in Europe a theatre of peace.

Since you may be unfamiliar with our Appeal, and our strategy, I will briefly rehearse these. We issued at the end of April 1980 an Appeal, over numerous and influential signatories in Western Europe and very few (although distinguished) signatories in the East. This warned of the near-approach of nuclear war, of the growth in the powers of military and of security services, and of the limitations imposed upon free exchanges of ideas and upon civil rights, in the West as well as in the East.

We affirmed the autonomy of the peace movement, as between the opposed blocs:

> We do not wish to apportion guilt between the political and military leaders of East and West. Guilt lies squarely upon both parties. Both parties have adopted meancing postures and committed aggressive actions in different parts of the world.

We proposed, then, as a common objective the expulsion of nuclear weapons and bases from the whole of Europe; the withdrawal of United States and Soviet nuclear weapons from European territory; the immediate halting of the deployment of the Soviet SS-20s and of the plans for cruise and Pershing missiles. We proposed, as means, a European-wide campaign, accompanied by every kind of exchange at every level, opening the whole continent to discourse and exchange of information. Explicitly, and with direct reference to civil rights, we said:

> We must defend and extend the right of all citizens, East or West, to take part in this common movement. . . We must commence to act as if a united, neutral and pacific Europe already exists. We must learn to be loyal, not to 'East' or 'West', but to each other, and we must disregard the prohibitions and limitations imposed by any national state.

Finally, we resumed once again the critical question of the peace movement's autonomy:

> We must resist any attempt by the statesmen of East or West to manipulate this movement to their own advantage. We offer no advantage to either NATO or the Warsaw alliance. Our objectives must be to free Europe from confrontation, to enforce detente between the United States and the Soviet Union, and ultimately, to dissolve both great power alliances.

This is what we said, and this is what we meant: both consciously and 'unconsciously' also. I do not suggest that the policy is perfect. I do not wish to avoid all argument. There are many problems: should our objective be a nuclear-weapons-free zone, from Poland to Portugal, or from the Atlantic to the Urals? Should we link conventional to nuclear armaments, and call for the withdrawal of both United States and Soviet conventional forces, under phased Rapacki-type agreements?

I argue only that the Appeal is a place where common action, and argument in good faith, can start. It is less a programme, once and for all, than a market-place around which a discourse of other arguments and proposals can take place. And, let us hope, a discourse of persons also: we envisage a European Convention, and perhaps also some great rally, or 'Theatre of Peace', at which citizens of East and West can enter into direct exchange.

As for our strategy, all that is open also. There is no hidden hand, no concealed 'vanguard', manipulating this movement, nor could there be. Our strategy is that of alliance. All persons, or parties, or churches, or societies, who support the objectives of the Appeal are associated, by that fact, with the common movement. We have no great bureaucracy, no extensive resources: whatever is done must be done by people themselves. Nor are we in a position to refuse any support, from whatever quarter. We cannot inspect persons, credentials nor impose a party line.

But we can and do hold firm to certain guiding principles. One (which I have stressed already) is the autonomy of the peace movement. Its allegiance is to neither bloc but to the remaking of a Europe of Peace.

A second is the principle of reciprocity. Whatever unilateral action any nation may take, in renouncing or refusing nuclear weapons and bases, this is to be seen as part of a continent-wide campaign, with demonstrations and other forms of symbolic expression, pressing reciprocal action upon the other powers. We are interested in discourse with various constituencies in 'the East', and we do not refuse dialogue with quasi-official bodies. But a condition for common action is that, whatever opposition they display towards Western nuclear 'modernisation' (an opposition which we share) they *also* signify and give expression to their opposition to Soviet 'modernisation': in particular, at this moment, to the deployment of the SS-20.

We appreciate that this is difficult. We have no expectations of CND-type marches and demonstrations. But we consider that, with patience and consultation, appropriate forms of expression will be found.

Third, we are committed, as an integral and necessary component of the idea of END, to breaking open a discourse throughout the whole continent—to the open exchange of persons and ideas, of information and also participation. We have said this again and again: this is no covert strategy. As I wrote, in the 'Notes' which you so much dislike, 'The rising movement in Western Europe against NATO "modernization" must exact a real price from the Soviet military managers, in the opening of Eastern Europe to genuine exchanges and to participation in the common internationalist discourse. This must not be a hidden tactic but an open and principled strategy.'

This entails a definite, but limited, commitment to the cause of civil rights. It is definite, because it is necessary to the movement's autonomy, and necessary also to the remaking of Europe. It is limited, in the sense that an autonomous peace movement cannot intervene in the particular cases and occasions of each nation's life (except where these concern the identity and relations of the peace movement itself), nor identity itself with sectional movements and programmes. As individuals, supporters of END can and do do more; as an autonomous movement of European repair, we cannot. You may find this ambiguous. But I have tried to be plain.

What, then, is your own strategy for the repair of Europe? I find, on this question, an inexplicable silence in your letter.

There is, at one point, a suggestion that the presence of ouı 'other world', the 'free West', acts in some way to 'restrain' your own totalitarian system. I can see that this may be so. The expression of Western public opinion may, in this or that case, have some marginal effect.

But can you seriously suppose that Western *war preparations* are conducive to the liberalisation of societies in the East? Can you explain to me how nuclear missiles and nerve gas contribute to human rights? Will any human rights survive a European 'theatre' war?

You argue against my view of an interactive process, by which the militarisation of each bloc enhances the militarisation of the other. Following Arendt, you find a sufficient explanation of Soviet militarisation in the original ill-will of Communist ideology: 'the suppression of human rights. . . manifests itself *also* in militarism'. Communist ideology is the self-sufficient author or its own military and security definitions of reality. And (perhaps?) only the noble nuclear weapons of the free West restrain it from world domination?

I think you are wrong, I think you are desperately mistaken. I wish we could spend three days together, and put your evidence and mine beside each other on the table.

There is, first, the point that, if this is the 'true' Communist idea, then it is not doing very well. There has not been, for very many years,any taste for that scenario in the West, whether 'Right' or 'Left'. Not even among Western Communist Parties–the powerful Eurocommunist tendency takes, as its starting-point, the absolute rejection of any such future.

A Communist 'idea' of world domination, which has lost Yugoslavia, which is losing Poland, which holds on with difficulty (and against the people) in Czechoslovakia and Hungary (and perhaps East Germany?), will face impossible problems of digestion if it seeks to swallow the Italians, the British, the French.

This is not a realistic proposal. It is an ideological fairy-tale, more to be expected as rhetorical decoration to the speeches of Western politicians than from the pen of an independent-minded writer in Prague.

On the contrary, I ask you to consider my own proposal once again. It is the military confrontation of the two blocs which continually refreshes the springs of totalitarianism, which legitimates the activities of the security services, which imposes military-ideological definitions of reality, which defines all dissent as 'treason' and as 'objectively' counter-revolutionary, which consolidates repressive state bureaucracies, which limits the space for human rights and which brings within its closure any hopeful social transition. As the missiles of the West press around the borders of the Soviet Union, they serve to hold together an authoritarian regime which has long lost all credibility; the utterly bankrupt ideology and methods of the Stalinist rear-guard are propped in place by each new military threat. And not only propped in place: it is a reciprocal, degenerative process. The succession to the old men of the Kremlin is being determined by the actions of the Pentagon today; and the Soviet Politbureau will be looking anxiously around for a strong man to answer General Haig.

How can this possibly help the advance of human rights? How has it helped in the past? Did it help the Hungarians in 1956? The Czechs in 1968? Are the threatening pronouncements of NATO Councils helping Polish Solidarity today? On the contrary: these enable *Rude Pravo* and *Isvestia* to denounce trade unionists and KOR advisers as 'counter-revolutionary elements', and to advance the arguments of military expediency to counter human rights.

Surely you must know by now, 'over there', that Western military pressure is empty, futile, and counterproductive? It is a bluff which has been thrice called: but, in calling it, the arguments of Communist orthodoxy and discipline have always emerged stronger. Throughout the past tense months, the space for Polish autonomy has been limited precisely by the *realpolitik* of the military confrontation. If the Polish people succeed in consolidating their new rights, it will owe everything to their own courage and discipline, nothing whatsoever to the Western military presence. What little help the West has been able to give to the Poles has been of a different, and more peaceful, kind: a little printing equipment, some delegations, a little trade union advice.

Would our own strategy, the strategy of END, have weakened the positions of Polish Solidarity? On the contrary. If, two years ago, acting together, we had succeeded in imposing some agreement upon both blocs–on the lines of the old Rapacki Plan–for the progressive demilitarisation of Poland and both Germanys, and for the pull-back of both American and Soviet forces, then surely the room for Polish autonomy would have been enlarged, and the dramas of the past months would have been less tense–and less hazardous, as they still remain?

I fear that the statesmen of the NATO powers care rather less for human rights than you suppose. We have opportunities for observing them which you do not. They are not conscience-struck about human rights in Chile, El Salvador, South Africa, Pakistan or Turkey. It is not in the nature of that kind of political beast to care very much about human liberties.

They are concerned in a different game, of interests and advantages. The rhetoric of human rights is serviceable enough. It allows for amazing propaganda victories, time after time, in the rhetorical Cold War. These victories, in turn, legitimate Western military dispositions and preparations.

But when a direct matter of interest is involved, then they care not at all. The more moderate and realistic Western advisers want, above all else, 'stability'. They want to congeal the *status quo:* they want the political map of Europe to remain the same for ever. They view the rash 'extremism' of Solidarity with anxiety: it offers to introduce 'instability' into the agreed hegemonic settlement of the affairs of Europe between both superpowers. The more hawkish and aggressive Western advisers are another matter again: they would like the combatants for human rights in Eastern Europe to make all the trouble for their rulers that they can. They *want* you to suffer, and to suffer *more.* This confirms their ideology and allows the military budgets to swell.

But they will not help you. They do not wish you to *win* your contests for human rights, because this would weaken their own ideological presuppositions. They wish you to trade your suffering and despair, for ever, into the coinage of the Cold War. The only help which they will bring you will be terminal: a European theatre war.

And why are we arguing? For there is one place in your letter where we stand close together: indeed, in an identical position. You write, 'Any disarmament movement is meaningful and hopeful only in the sense of the realisation of its objectives as a human rights movement.'

This is exactly where END started, and where we still stand. We wish to set in motion an alternative logic of process. We wish to bring into a common understanding, a common perspective of European solidarity, the Western movement for peace and the Eastern movement for civil, trade union and intellectual rights.

Why then does your letter reveal so many and so deep suspicions of us and our motives?

You offer only one reason, and it is one which I respect. You view with suspicion a limited and mercenary notion of 'detente', which is confined to economic agreements at the level of state self-interests, and which (you argue) can simply be turned to the advantage of the rulers of the Warsaw bloc. I accept this warning. But it is not the same as the policy of END. We propose direct exchanges, the opening of discourse and common action between the citizenry of East and West, which may, at the same time, strengthen the causes both of peace and of civil rights, and offer some protection to combatants for democratic rights in the East.

I think it probable that the real grounds of your suspicions are different. And I will suggest three.

First, the incessant official 'peace-loving' propaganda of your own rulers induces in you such nausea that the very word 'peace' has become, for you, an object of suspicion. It is a rhetoric in whose name every measure of repression goes forward.

I understand your reaction. There is a glossy, mendacious publication of 'friendship' in this country called *Czechoslovak Life.* I have before me, in an issue of June 1980, a pompous address by Vasil Bilak, Secretary of the Central Committee of the CPC, entitled 'Socialism and Peace are Inseparable'.

The role of Bilak, during the Prague crisis of 1968, has been sufficiently exposed by Mlynar. I will only add that it therefore did not surprise me that Mr Bilak in the accompanying photograph has exactly the same furtive and shifty expression as President Nixon wore during the Watergate scandal.

I understand, perfectly, why such 'peaceloving' professions make you sick. I have been told that certain members of the official Czech Peace Committee had the integrity to protest at the events of 1968. They were all summarily dismissed and a new 'Peace Committee' appointed in their place. If this is true, then END has no desire to speak with that 'Peace Committee'.

This, then, is understood. But you should not allow the good name of peace to be expropriated so easily. Mr Bilak (I notice) claims also as the property of his side the causes of 'liberty and human rights'. Have you therefore turned your back upon these?

Second, I suspect that your response to END is influenced by slight and partial information. You suppose that the movement has been launched, in the West, by naive persons of 'goodwill' and fellow-travellers. You have perhaps been told that the initiators are such people.

I will only say, then, that the initiators and the majority of the signatories to the END Appeal are persons who have, over many years, clearly identified their support for the cause of civil rights in Eastern Europe. My own unequivocal commitment to this cause goes back, it is true, for only twenty-five years; but other initiators have a longer record than that. And the Bertrand Russell Peace Foundation, which has been the centre for distribution of the Appeal and correspondence throughout Europe, has repeatedly supported, through publications, public meetings, and petitions the cause of Soviet and Eastern European 'dissidents', and of Charter 77 in particular.

You may enquire into these credentials more closely if you wish. But a third reason for your suspicions may perhaps be more complex, and less pleasant, than this. You may even have been in receipt—in all innocence—of 'disinformation'.

I was surprised, when conversing with friends in Prague, to learn that among visitors who passed between the West and your city were certain persons who, very probably, are in the service of Western intelligence.

I ought not to have been surprised. This is, of course, very much part of the Cold War game. Nor do I think it to be a very sensational or scandalous matter. These persons are not in the business of 'conspiracy' or 'sabotage'; they are simply tedious people amassing files and trivial information.

From what we read these days in our own press, it would seem that the work of 'Intelligence' is a good deal more futile and unintelligent than is supposed. The major occupation of the rival intelligence services appears to be mutual interpenetration; and while there may be much to be said for this occupation when it takes place between lovers, one supposes that it provides less gratification when the partners are the KGB, MI6 and CIA.

There is nothing very desperate, nor even efficient, about these people, and we must not allow ourselves to be reduced by them to conspiracy or paranoia. And yet there is one objective to which both Western and Eastern security services are committed in common. *They do not wish the democratic movements of the East and West to recognise each other and to make common cause.* That would destroy their whole game: it would put them out of business altogether. They wish each of us to suspect the other, and to go on trading ourselves into the currency of the Cold War.

I suspect that a little 'disinformation' is going on in Eastern Europe today, as to the policy of END and the motives of its initiators. It might come, equally well, from the 'Intelligence' of West or East: very probably the former. I ask you to pause before you accept such information, and to enquire, rather closely, into its veracity.

I am, as I get older, more and more of an anti-statist: I do not trust state power. I had formed, some years ago, a conclusion not unlike that which concludes your own letter. What matter most are not the stereotypes of 'Left' and 'Right' but the active democratic values and respect for persons and for human rights. If I have a quarrel with you, it is this. You are a libertarian and anti-statist, but only on your side of the world. I ask you to extend your anti-statism a little further: and to show less confidence in the states of the West.

Either we will burn together, East and West, or we must reverse the inexorable thrust towards war. And we can do that only by making Europe whole once more, by healing the open wound which runs across the heart of our continent. Nothing less than a new internationalism, a commitment to each other, will be enough.

The opposed military blocs can never be such healers. For they operate, by definition, upon the principles of human fission.

We are in search of the alternative forces of fusion. It is (we agree) a difficult, an improbable, strategy. It would commence, at first, with a few exchanges, with a dialogue; it might find expression, among the youth of both halves of Europe, in some common symbols and symbolic actions; it would rest, not upon uniform programmes, but upon a mutual understanding of each other's objectives.

But if those two forces could be brought together in solidarity and fusion–autonomous, democratic, and anti-militarist–then an immense and affirmative presence would be felt across the whole continent. It is the only presence which could possibly be powerful enough to prevent the logic of militarism from reaching its ultimate consummation. But if that presence should assert itself, then, in the same moment, the very parameters of Cold War politics (which have endured now for over thirty years) would be transformed. Small nations would reassume autonomy, new spaces for social experiment would open up, a new discourse of persons and of ideas would commence.

You may think this to be impossible. But we are glad that you opened this exchange, and we will welcome your response. We wish you success in your contest for human rights, including (not least) your right to disagree with us.

Yours sincerely,

E.P. Thompson

CAMPAIGNING FOR EUROPEAN NUCLEAR DISARMAMENT (END)

A SHOW FOR THE EUROPEAN THEATRE?

I have been teaching and peace-working in the United States for five months, and the scene is frightening. Middle America has got itself into a Suez mood, and Reagan was floated to power on a tide of Know-Nothing nationalist sentiment unloosed by totally irresponsible media.

The burden of it all is this: America has been humiliated, first in Vietnam, then by a bunch of Iranian fanatics. America is being pushed around. The American armed forces are falling apart. The Russians have stolen a lead in arms. No one pushes Americans around. Reagan is going to stop that and go for US superiority. US technology is still the Greatest, and now it is time to use it. The first Commie or wog to get in Reagan's way and—WHAM!

This surge of nationalism is combined with an utterly unrealistic, indeed isolationist world-view: it is a sort of psychological isolationism armed with nukes. War is, always, something for export—'over there'. It seems that few Americans, outside the liberal enclaves, understand that in any superpower conflict the North American continent will share in the common incineration.

I found three things especially frightening. First, there is an ugly hysteria about oil. Americans have been sold the notion that the Persian Gulf is an American sea, and that the Russians are poised to cut their jugular vein.

(Yet the US has huge stockpiles of oil, little over 10 per cent of US oil consumption comes from the Middle East, and this could easily, with benefit, be saved by a little conservation.)

Europeans are chided for being slow to prepare military

From the *Guardian*, 23 February 1981.

interventions in the Middle East. We are now being asked to harbour in Europe (and contribute forces to) the US rapid deployment force of 100,000 men poised to defend the jugular vein. From the standpoint of the Middle East, 'defence' and good old imperialist aggression look much the same.

Second, there is an ugly desire to push Europe around, to bring the NATO states into more obedient clientage (paying more for their 'defence'), and to harden all East-West oppositions. During the long Polish crisis of this winter it became clear that the NATO hawks actually *wanted* Soviet military intervention in Poland. They were panting for the Russians to come, so as to legitimate a huge upping in military expenditure, and so as to confirm their own worst-case ideology. They need Russian actions of a kind to justify their own.

Third, and most threatening, is the confirmation of that process of the 'deep structuring' of the armaments race which I argued in *Protest and Survive.* Like actors summoned to cue, there enter now on the world stage Vice-President Bush (from the CIA) and General Haig, from NATO Command.

Democratic opposition to Haig's appointment centred on his seamy record in the Watergate affair. Less was said as to his role as the architect of the NATO 'modernisation' project. Haig has been not only a theorist of 'theatre war' but has actually directed a dry run for such a war in NATO's 'Wintex' exercises of 1977. As Supreme Allied Commander, Europe, he then signed the order for a NATO first nuclear strike to 'convey a decisive escalation of sufficient shock to convincingly persuade the enemy' to withdraw. More was to be split in this strike than a mere infinitive. The General nominated as targets five airfields in East Germany and five in Bulgaria, and three each in Czechoslovakia, Poland and Hungary, as well as sundry troop assembly and supply areas for further strikes. Russia was not to be struck, the first time around.

This is the man who now is architect of US diplomacy. According to this scenario, after this first ('persuasive') strike, the President and the First Secretary will get together on the hot line and will agree to call the whole thing off.

Everything that walks or grows or flies or swims on this planet will be at the mercy of the decision of two panic-struck silly old men.

And now General Haig's loyal successor, General Rogers, comes forward to sell us the neutron bomb. The cuddly, chuckling general was afforded prime TV time to explain, with a glint in his eye, how he, as a military man, needed (oh, so much!) this sweet piece of hardware, because he could then put it down among the enemy software, but in safety, only a few hundred yards in front of his own. But, of course (chuckle, chuckle) it was only a 'deterrent': the whole point of making it was it would never be used.

The stench of these megadeaths, only a little way ahead of us in the future, is beginning to drift back into our present time. We begin to rise from our seats, in the European theatre, and make for the exits. But each time we try to move, in West Europe, the exits are blocked by those monstrous SS-20s. Have you noticed how they are multiplying, if not on the ground, then certainly in the Western official hand-outs? And multiplying perhaps they are. United States militarism looks so ugly at the moment—and its diplomacy so irresponsible—that it is possible for some in the Western peace movement to forget that Soviet militarism is ugly also. The upthrust of weaponry is reciprocal: the hawks continue to breed each others' hawks.

Last autumn I spoke at a large and friendly meeting in Manhattan's Riverside Church—a church with an outstanding record of work for international reconciliation. In a smaller discussion meeting afterwards, a well-briefed Russian (I think a Georgian) announced himself as a secretary of the World Peace Council. In an eloquent and peace-loving statement he commended me for my correct delineation of the aggressive strategies of NATO, but then explained, very patiently, that I was mistaken in calling on the Soviet Union also to halt deployment of SS-20s. After all that I had said about NATO's menacing strategies I would surely agree that this was 'quite impossible'? The SS-20s were absolutely 'necessary' for the Warsaw powers' 'defence'.

I told him that he was arguing as a nationalist and not as an internationalist; that his arguments were the mirror-image of those of NATO apologists; and that, very certainly, the Soviet Union could take unilateral action, today, to halt or to reduce its SS-20s without endangering its security one iota. Moreover, no action would contribute more to the strengthening of the peace movement (and its arguments) throughout all Europe than this.

I think it is of great importance, at this moment of growth in the Western European movement, for us to keep steadily in view the strategy (however difficult) of bringing pressure upon *both* sides to disarm. I shall oppose cruise and Trident whether or not the SS-20 is dismantled: these are evil and they bring us into greater danger. But our movement cannot succeed unless we can break, somehow, across that divide, and call forth reciprocal responses from the East. To allow the Western peace movement to drift into collusion with the strategy of the World Peace Council—that is, in effect, to become a movement opposing NATO militarism *only*—is a recipe for our own containment and ultimate defeat. This will also meet with a refusal in those parts of Eastern Europe (Czechoslovakia, Poland) where much public opinion is utterly jaded with official 'peace-loving' propaganda, and where state-sponsored Peace Committees have never, throughout their whole 30-year existence, fluttered an eyelash in protest against any action of Soviet militarism.

The European Appeal insisted upon the need for lateral exchanges between citizens, by-passing the organs of the State; and insisted also upon the necessity for open exchanges of information and proposals between East and West. This entails a clear general commitment to the cause of civil rights and open communication in the East. Only in this way can the tissues begin to heal across East and West. Peace and democracy have to go together.

NEUTRALISM AND INTERNATIONALISM

A new character has entered upon the European stage. She, or he, arrived nameless, some time last spring, preceded by tens of thousands of marching feet and banners. The media scratched their multiple heads and decided to give the new arrival a name: 'Neutralism'.

Neutralism, in fact, does not often give *itself* this name. But the media know best, especially in America. Last week 'neutralism' even hit the pages of *Newsweek, Time magazine,* and *Maclean's* (where I found out that I was a 'guru' of European neutralism).

The odd thing is that Neutralism (or whatever it is) is never allowed to speak in its own voice. You will not find the leading exponents of European disengagement, or of a nuclear-weapons-free Europe (which are not exactly the same thing as neutralism) being interrogated deferentially on the BBC: I am thinking of such people as Alva Myrdal, the Swedish expert on disarmament; Professor Ulrich Albrecht, of the Free University of West Berlin; Mient Jan Faber of the Dutch Interchurch Peace Council (IKV); Dr Albert de Smaele, the veteran Belgian politician; Rudolf Bahro, the East German utopian theorist; or Ken Coates of the Bertrand Russell Peace Foundation.

'Neutralism' is first given that label *by* the media: and then it is gestured at, abused, caricatured ('better-red-than-deadism'), or nodded towards in a knowing way. The nearest we have as yet got to any presentation of it was a crisp piece of TV journalism (BBC Newsweek) by Steve Brashaw. This *described* some of the things the West European peace movement is now doing, in an agile and interesting way. But

---

From the *Guardian*, 31 August 1981.

why we are doing them, what our *objectives* are, went unexamined. Worse, these were assumed within the terms of the presenter's own Cold War premises: 'a majority of Europeans may prefer the Librium of neutralism to the expensive, risky defence of that state of affairs which, in surer times, everyone agreed to call liberty. . .' Fade out to misty stars-and-stripes against the Berlin wall, and (margin, off-left) neutralist banners waving in abject submission to massing SS-20s and Soviet tanks.

But Neutralism (or whatever it is) may not even cough and clear its throat in public. That is very odd, in Western democracies, and when 'a majority of Europeans' may even be in favour of it. Of what?

The most sensational accounts of European 'neutralism' are now being made by the American media which, having ignored the peace movement for twelve months, suddenly reversed engines. They are not quite sure which story-line to follow. On the one hand, Europeans are victims of a massive 'Soviet peace offensive', 'a well-orchestrated propaganda campaign based in Moscow' (thus Caspar Weinberger). On the other hand, Europeans are running scared, have gone 'soft' on Russia, and are going in for 'appeasement' or a self-regarding pacifism which tries to 'opt out' of the Western Alliance–while still expecting the USA to pay for their 'defence'. Both story-lines can be put together, for Moscow can 'orchestrate' the softies.

These are dangerous people: Caspar Weinberger, Richard Allen, Lawrence Eagleburger, and all those advisers now grouped around President Reagan–men with minds like delivery-systems, whose knowledge of Europe is minimal, who are too busy to read what Europeans say, and who have time only to scan a page or two of briefing as they fly from one planning meeting to the next. 'Neutralism? O.K. We'll toughen up those Euro-softies.'

These people need the Cold War, and they need to soup it up. They are determined to get their new hardware down: cruise missiles, the neutron bomb, nerve gas, the MX: their attitude to negotiations is strictly cosmetic and propagandist. There are only Two Camps: the USA (sometimes known, for some archaic reason, as 'the Free World') versus Communist terrorism. Anyone who resists their objectives must be neutralist, and neutralists must be pro-Soviet.

These dangerous people actually *want* the Russians to intervene in Poland, because this would open every door to the militarisation of the West. I did not make this up. In a closely-researched article in the *New York Sunday Times* (July 12, 1981) Leslie Gelb interrogated Reagan's advisers, in 'off-the-record' briefings with 'high-ranking' State Department and Defense spokesmen.

> The last thing Reagan officials say they want to do is calm public opinion. As several of these officials explained it, to calm public opinion in Europe and the United States would be to lull the people again into a false sense of security and undercut pressure for increased military spending. Some high-ranking officials in the Reagan Administration say that if the Russians did invade Poland it would at least make clear who the good guys and bad guys were and would mobilise the West.

The point is, not whether 'neutralism' in some form may or may not be a viable policy for particular nations, but what meaning the Weinberger/Allen lobby is trying to attribute to the term: neutralism-as-librium. I have myself, for over twenty years, written in favour of *active* or *positive* neutrality. (The second term is of Yugoslav provenance, in the days of the Tito-Nehru-Nasser non-alignment policy.) The emphasis, here, has been as much on the adjective as on the noun, and it has carried the connotations of a third, non-aligned, way between the opposed superpowers and blocs.

From my knowledge of the growing European peace movements I would say that 'neutralism-as-librium', or as self-regarding opting-out, scarcely has *any* advocates among them. Their stance is far more active and internationalist than that. And first of all (if I may brief Mr Weinberger) I do not know what 'orchestrated' means.

I look out of my window at the Worcestershire country-side, and I really do not know how I came to be orchestrated by Moscow, nor by what route my score has come. In fact, the European peace movements are not yet orchestrated at all. I would describe them as an orchestra still in the process of assembling, with fragments of a common score, and with no conductor.

The scene is vigorous but confused. In the Nordic countries there is now a formidable lobby for a Scandinavian nuclear-weapons-free zone: but this need not necessarily involve the detachment of Denmark or Norway from NATO. In south-east Europe a similar lobby is growing. In mid-October there will be elections in Greece, and PASOK, led by Andreas Papandreou, may win a majority. PASOK is committed to opposition to American bases and to Greek membership of NATO; if he wins, Papandreou will become, like Allende before him, a candidate for destabilisation and will need all-European support.

There is a growing lobby to keep Spain out of NATO, but in Italy the Communist Party is pro-NATO, although it is moving (under pressure from its youth) in a ponderous and gingerly way into opposition to cruise missiles. (The Sicilian cooperative farmers, who are having cruise missiles dumped among them, are likely to react more energetically, as the Larzac shepherds have done in France, in their long and successful campaign to defend their grazing lands from the military.)

Meanwhile in Holland, Belgium, Britain and West Germany there are powerful, 'unilateralist', CND-type movements, which express total opposition to any new measures of militarisation. There are also political parties, churches, and pressure groups, each with an individual accent.

This is orchestrated nothing. It is a huge tuning of instruments, which reached a new level with the great Hamburg 'Protestant Day' on June 20, and will reach a new level again with the demonstrations in Bonn (October 10th) and London (October 24th). The words that one reaches for are not 'neutralism', but diversity, disengagement, a third way, or European internationalism. If there is any common notion that is beginning to conduct the ensemble it is that of peaceful European opinion acting as a Third Negotiator, between both superpowers, with the ultimate objective of reunifying European societies and culture.

'Neutralism' in its current media designation, commences within the premises of the Cold War and assumes that no other premises are possible. It is predicated upon that facile division of the world into binary antinomies which has so often tricked the human mind: good/bad, the damned and the saved. It is a kind of Cold War Calvinism.

It assumes that diplomacy *must* be carried on according to the rules (of 'balance', deterrence and 'posture') laid down by the superpowers, and that anyone who tries to play any different game must be 'neutral'. The curious thing is that the Cold War ideologists of both sides want the game to go on; and both are impatient of a European peace movement which refuses to take one side or the other. Both lots then shout out 'Foul!' 'Neutralism!' Neutral *to us!*

I suppose that one can call the European peace movements neutral, in the sense that they refuse to play this game at all; I would prefer the term 'non-aligned'. But what is of interest about them is not the old game which they are *not* playing, but the new games which they are trying to invent.

This diverse tuning-up of European peaceful opinion is searching for new and active measures to break up the old Cold War structures; and reviving old proposals for local European disengagement (like the Rapacki plan) in new forms. It is looking, not only for a third way, but for fourth and fifth ways: one way for Finland, another for Greece, and others again for Holland and Poland–each one of them adding to the common pressure to free the continent from nuclear weapons and bases, to make a calm space between the superpowers, and to permit smaller nations, East or West, to resume their own initiatives.

I could provide plenty of chapter-and-verse, from Scandinavian, German or Dutch sources, to confirm my account of the dominant thinking in the European peace movements. These unorchestrated movements are neither pro-Soviet nor are they in support of 'neutralism-as-librium': they are exploring areas of disengagement, they are pressing for reciprocal initiatives from the East. They favour the loosening of both blocs and they also, significantly, favour the cause of civil rights in East Europe. They are putting the cause of peace and the cause of liberty together.

CND DEMONSTRATION

This has been an extraordinary year of campaigning. We have multiplied our numbers. We have carried conferences—the Labour party, the Liberal party, the TUC and many others. We have won the argument in the country and carried it to every town and to small villages.

We have done this despite the opposition of arrogant rulers, editors and bureaucrats, who pretend to represent the consensus of this country. There is no such consensus. We have torn that official fiction up. On our leading demands—opposition to cruise missiles, to Trident, support for a Nuclear-free Europe—it is we who represent majority opinion in this country.

Let the world understand, from our numbers here today, that the British government, in its military policies, no longer represents the British people. If the Tories will not turn from these policies, then they will not in this generation ever be returned.

In 1983 or 4—if not earlier—two public nuisances will be rejected and sent packing: cruise missiles and Mrs Thatcher's government. The lady's not for returning.

Last year in Trafalgar Square I asked you to look around you and sense your own strength. Today I ask you to look further: beyond the margins of Hyde Park. . . to your fellow marchers and peace workers in Bonn, in Athens, in Scandinavia, in Brussels, throughout Holland.

This is the astonishing achievement of one year. We now have friends and allies, working towards our common objective of sweeping all nuclear weapons from our continent, throughout northern, western and southern Europe. They

---

Speech at Hyde Park, 24 October 1981.

are already influencing practical politics. There are now practical possibilities for establishing a Nordic Nuclear-free Zone. I have been this week speaking in Norway and Denmark, at the invitation of our friends, the 'No to Nuclear Weapons' movements–and in Copenhagen and Oslo I was asked by large meetings to bring their greetings to you at this meeting today.

Last week in Greece a fateful event took place for all Europe: the victory of PASOK. PASOK and its leader Mr Papandreou are committed to the cause of END. The new Greek government intends to work at once for a Nuclear-Free Zone in the Balkans, taking in nations from NATO (Greece), from the Warsaw Pact (Roumania and Bulgaria) and non-aligned Yugoslavia. Through all Europe our movement must defend this great opening to peace: we must not permit anyone to destabilise PASOK nor to make of Papandreou another Allende. We must demand upon both NATO and the Warsaw powers–no intervention in either Greece or Poland. Let Poland be Polish and let Greece be Greek!

Nordic–Balkan–and now to Central Europe. Two weeks ago 300,000 Germans–young, peaceful, determined–demonstrated in Bonn. This is a new Germany and this Germany also is demanding a Nuclear-free Europe, East as well as West. Our greetings and our solidarity to them!

In the coming year we must strengthen our links with this European movement–exchange delegations, confer, invite their speakers, support each others demonstrations. Out of the common threat to our continent we are creating a new internationalism.

And we must look even further. We must look across the Atlantic to our fellow peace workers in America and Canada. We already owe them much. Their courageous journalists, scientists and peace workers have kept open the channels of communication–they have told the world the truth about nuclear weapons. We salute them in their churches and universities–George Kennan, the physicians, the distinguished American speakers now in this country.

In the other direction we look towards the Soviet Union and Eastern Europe. Here is another task for the coming year. It is not an easy one. It is easy for official spokespersons for the Warsaw bloc to voice opposition to Western missiles. What we are waiting for is some opposition to their own.

The peace movement in Western Europe is non-aligned. It is opposed to militarisation, West or East. That was the message of the great demonstration in Bonn. That is the message of this demonstration also. We demand the halting of NATO's plans for new missiles, unconditionally. There is no need for negotiations. We demand also the halting and the reduction in numbers of the SS-20s. Unconditionally, without negotiations. That is the way to get multilateral disarmament–take two unilateral initiatives and put them together.

We ask the Soviet TV and Press who are present here to report our demands fully to the Soviet people. Don't tell them there was a great meeting in London to protest against NATO's plans. That's only half the truth. Tell them there was a meeting to get nuclear weapons out of our whole continent. Including the SS-20s. And that this meeting is calling, now, upon the people of the Soviet Union and of Eastern Europe to join hands in this common struggle–not only against NATO's modernisation but also against their own.

This is the task before us in 1982. We have to go behind the missiles to the Cold War itself. So long as Europe is divided into two hostile blocs they will go on inventing new and more hideous weapons.

We have got to put Europe back together, East and West. This is the historic task of the peace movement. This can't be done by the victory of one side over the other, but only by a movement of peoples against the military and security systems of both sides. We have to dig a hundred different channels of discourse *beneath* the States–doctors, churches, universities, Trade Unionists, women's organisations. Nuclear-free cities in Britain must find out twins in Eastern Europe. The peace movement must begin to cross the East-West frontier.

My last word is to the young people here. This is, above all, your work, your historic task. Across our whole continent, young people are rejecting the black clouds inherited from 35 years ago. Just as they have rejected racism, the young are turning their backs upon exterminism, and its barbarous symbols of 'deterrence'. It is you who must invent the features of a peaceful Europe, beyond the Cold War–you must invent the new symbols and logos, the sounds, the living theatre of peace, the new vocabulary of internationalism.

And you must do it soon. We have multiplied our numbers. We have won our arguments. But we have not yet stopped one missile in its tracks. The whole grotesque carnival of annihilation is still on the road–cruise, Pershing, SS-20, Backfire, Trident, Minuteman, MX, Polaris, Poseidon. . . Time is not on our side.

ZERO OPTION: A NUCLEAR-FREE EUROPE

On Wednesday of last week President Reagan proposed what was described as a 'zero option'. Within minutes the telephone was ringing and I was being asked, not only from Britain but from the USA and Canada, what I—or 'the peace movement'—or 'the European peace movement' thought about it.

This is rather a silly carry-on. Mr Reagan, his advisers, the Defence Ministers of NATO powers, are briefed by armies of subordinates, confer at Gleneagles, get their PR operations and lobbies prepared. . . and then 'the peace movement', which consists of a few Personalities singled out for media attention, two or three small over-pressed offices, and thousands of overworked voluntary activists, is expected to utter its common mind, at the drop of a hat.

This cannot be done. We also have to consult and to find a common mind. I cannot speak for 'the peace movement'. I can only give an interim personal opinion.

I recall saying on the phone, first, that Reagan's proposals indicated an extraordinary change in tone from anything we had heard from his administration in the past 10 months: that this was a direct response to the pressure of the European peace movement, and to the troubles of his allies, including Chancellor Schmidt. I welcomed this. I then said that the actual proposals were in many ways one-sided but that the response of the peace movement should be positive—we should press for *more*.

On Friday I set off with a small British delegation on a long-planned consultation with German friends. On Sunday

---

From the *Guardian*, 30 November 1981, with minor revisions.

(22 November) we got the *Observer* in Bonn and read an article by Mr John Nott, the Secretary of State for Defence:

> Within minutes of the President's speech we heard not only the applause we would expect, but also the clamour of some commentators vying with each other to dissect the offer and show, not its undoubted value, but where it might founder. Professor Thompson was quickly on television. It did not make sense, he argued.

Wrong on three counts, Mr Nott. I am not a professor. I did not go on television. And that was not my response. Why should our Secretary of State invent this story? Or was he briefed by a disinformer? And if he is briefed so badly on British matters, what must we conclude about his briefing on Russian?

The next day, in Berlin, Daniel Ellsberg got hold of the *Guardian.* He pointed out to me your correspondent's report of meetings in Bonn, the previous day, on the occasion of Brezhnev's visit:

> The Greens, with Professor [again!] E.P. Thompson, Mr Daniel Ellsberg and Rudolf Bahro, were calling for peace without mentioning freedom. Many of them spoke out against Mr Brezhnev's visit and said that all nuclear arms were bad. But their main point remains that American arms were far worse than the Soviet Union's and President Reagan's 'zero option' was an illusory offer and a deliberate deception put forward as a way of increasing the arms race.

Our hosts at this meeting in Bonn were the 'Greens'. They had planned a discussion meeting on the theme of 'What should the peace movement ask of the Soviet Union?' The fly-sheet advertising the meeting stressed the common interests shared between the movements for civil and trade union rights in the East and for peace in the West. It was *all* about freedom.

It was an untidy, unplanned meeting with a score of speakers. 'Without mentioning freedom'??!!! The speakers included a representative of the Afghan Social-Democratic party, a Soviet emigré, Rudolf Bahro (who, not long ago, was imprisoned in East Germany), Erich Fried (the Austrian poet), and Zdenek Mlynar (Dubcek's former colleague and author of *Night Frost in Prague*).

No-one 'spoke out against' Brezhnev's visit: most spoke about the Soviet military-ideological bureaucracy and how it might be influenced. All demanded freer exchange of information, and contacts between citizens, East and West. Some speakers said that Reagan's offer was illusory (a view strongly held in the German peace movement). But it is false (and damaging) to imply that Daniel Ellsberg made this analysis. On the contrary, he made a new and striking constructive proposal, to which I will return.

Why should these inventions have been published at this moment? I can only suppose that certain people are less interested in getting rid of missiles than in getting rid of the peace movement. They wish it to be assumed that the peace movement must be pro-Russian and that any disarmament proposal from Reagan must take the wind out of its sails. And if it is pro-Russian then of course it cannot 'mention' freedom. Evidence is then invented to fit the case, and is fed as disinformation to unwary politicians and journalists.

Yet at the same time quite contrary disinformation was being spread. At the great Dortmund rally, the first anniversary of the 'Krefeld Appeal', I said–in the face of some opposition–that the response of the peace movement to such a change in tone from President Reagan must be positive: we must hold to our own unilateral positions, but we must say 'yes' to negotiations: 'Yes, but *more*.'

It was then reported in the Dutch press that I had urged the acceptance of Reagan's 'zero option'. This provoked consternation and enquiry from our friends in the Dutch Interchurch Peace Council. Yet in the *International Herald Tribune* (November 24) it was reported that the Dutch Council had agreed to 'a moderation' of its 'campaign against nuclear weapons in Western Europe'. This provoked consternation and enquiry in the peace movement over here. Both statements were false. Both could have arisen from confusion. Or both could be part (to borrow the language of our opponents) of an orchestrated campaign, centred on Washington, to confuse and divide the European movements.

It is spooky to find oneself being moved around the propaganda board in one's own absence. I would prefer to address these questions in my own voice, even if consultation with my colleagues, in Britain and in Europe, is far from complete.

First, I repeat that Reagan's proposals signify a remarkable change in tone. This change is a response to us. And our response to that change must be positive also. How can a peace movement give a negative response to *any* proposals to reduce nuclear weapons? We must say: 'Yes, but more!'

We must also make a positive response to Brezhnev's proposals to freeze and to commence a unilateral reduction in numbers of SS-20s, while negotiations go ahead. We–END, the Dutch Interchurch Peace Council–have long been asking the Soviet Union to do exactly that, unconditionally, in advance of negotiations. This should have been done months ago. Once again, we should say: 'Yes, but more!'

But, second, the peace movement must stand at right-angles to the arguments of 'balance'. Reagan's and Brezhnev's proposals are only the opening salvos of an artillery exchange of propaganda which may continue for months. It will be tempting to be drawn into the numbers game–so many SS-20s = so many forward-based NATO systems. If we fall for this, the peace movement will be swiftly divided–some for Reagan, some for Brezhnev, some in-between–and all will have bargained away their unilateralist birthright for a mess of superpower pottage.

In these times of grotesque overkill, the arguments of balance are trivial at every level except that of 'face'. If there are enough nuclear weapons now in Europe to destroy the continent thirty times over, what does it matter if one side can do it 14 times and the other 16? What matters is to put the process into reverse.

And we have, already, started to do that in Europe, not by prolonged negotiation, but by public pressure and argument. It was very grand of Reagan to announce to the world that, in certain circumstances, he would cancel cruise and Pershing II. He was offering, as a bargaining-chip, a gift which is not, and never will be, in his power to make–*our* land as a site for *his* missiles.

Whether these missiles come upon our territories or not is a decision to be made by the European peoples most concerned. It is not to be made in Washington, nor in Geneva (where there is no European seat at the table). In effect, the Dutch and Belgian people have already withdrawn their permission, unilaterally: and the permission of the British, German and Italian people is in doubt. Reagan and Brezhnev are under a great illusion, if they think they have some right to balance *us* in the scales of *their* nuclear lunacy.

Do my two points contradict each other? No, because the peace movement's position is, like that of NATO, double-track. One track: we push the nuclear weapons powers (including our own) to reverse the arms drive, to negotiate, to reach reciprocal agreements. As a 'Third Negotiator' we monitor their proceedings, expose their propaganda falsehoods, and insert our own independent proposals. But our second track remains unilateral: cruise and Pershing II will not come, Polaris and the F-111 must go.

The NATO double track, which Chancellor Schmidt has been explaining to Mr Brezhnev last week, is this. NATO will negotiate the most advantageous agreement possible in terms of 'balance'; if this fails, then NATO will deploy the new missiles anyway. The position of the peace movement is the same, but in reverse. We will press both sides to agree on the largest possible measures of reciprocal disarmament; and if they try to introduce the new missiles, we will refuse them anyway.

Let me offer my own thoughts, as a monitor, on the first track. Reagan's proposals have been called 'the zero option', but they come in an odd form, as a *minus*-zero option.

An earlier 'zero option', proposed by Willy Brandt, suggested a sharp cut in SS-20s in exchange for cancelling NATO's 'modernisation'. The reasoning was this: the Soviet Union was planning to withdraw all of its obsolescent SS-4s and SS-5s, and replace these with SS-20s. Brandt's version of the 'zero option' would have permitted them to keep as many of the three-headed SS-20s as would replace the older missiles, but no more. In terms of the 'balance' game, this would have meant reverting to the old position before 1979.

Reagan, with the support of Herr Genscher (the West German Defence Minister), has now pushed this deep cut down to *nil* SS-20s, plus the removal of all of the old weapons. This may be regarded either as a tough negotiating posture or as a provocation. The SS-4s and 5s have been around since the early 1960s (the first ones were emplaced in 1959), and, as Dr Gregory Treverton of the International Institute of Strategic Studies has noted (*Nuclear Weapons in Europe,* Adelphi Papers no. 168) 'for most of the 1960s and 1970s this threat received little attention and seemed to cause little concern'.

These weapons are, of course, a foul threat, just as are Polaris, Poseidon and the F-111s. The peace movement must never be pushed into a corner ('balance', 'deterrence') in which it seems to be defending any of them. Yet grossly one-sided proposals, introduced with massive media hoo-ha ('an historic offer', says Mr Nott, who has just ordered Trident), are a threat also, since they block effective negotiations and can even be cosmetics daubed upon the nuclear death's-head.

For this reason, if the SS-4s and 5s are to be included in the bargain, then some NATO systems (including the Pershing IA) ought also to be traded in. If Mr Nott really wishes to make 'an historic offer', he might put his Polaris on the table also. That might remove one block.

Then the answer of the peace movement to Reagan should still be: 'Yes, but more.' How much more, of what? Others have suggested shopping-lists. It is up for discussion, not only in Washington or behind closed doors at Gleneagles, but across our continent.

Daniel Ellsberg, of *The Pentagon Papers,* brought forward a striking new proposal at Bonn. He has already made it public, and I hope I can explain it with his own clarity. It is this. President Reagan's proposals could be accepted, without further bargaining, if–but only if–they are accompanied at once by a general freeze, binding upon all powers, upon the deployment, manufacture, development and testing of all further nuclear weapons at every level.

His reasoning is this. First, the cruise and Pershing II missiles are immensely threatening. They must be stopped. There are powerful interests in the Pentagon and NATO determined to go ahead with their deployment, which resisted up to the last minute the 'zero option' even in its minus form. These *want* the Soviet Union to reject the proposals, and will do everything possible to switch back to the other track.

To stop these missiles will be a major step, and a victory for the peace movement also. Even in terms of 'balance', the other side should be willing to buy this victory with large concessions.

But, second, hard-nosed Soviet advisers will have good reasons to smell a trap in any proposal limited to intermediate weapons (and only ground-launched ones at that) from an administration which has a vast ongoing rearmament programme in strategic and tactical nuclear weapons. They have been tricked before, when SALT I negotiated 'parity' in delivery-systems and then the United States introduced MIRVs (multiple independently-targeted re-entry vehicles), and multiplied the warheads on each missile overnight.

The obvious trick this time would be to remove cruise missiles from the territory of Europe, where their political cost is becoming too high, and put them down in the Eastern Atlantic instead. And this is already being prepared. Caspar Weinberger has already ordered several thousand cruise missiles, some air-launched, some submarine-launched, others to be placed on great launching-platforms—old World War II warships taken out of mothballs, their decks cleared as floating-launchers.

Plans announced in Washington on October 2nd, 1981, included several hundreds of cruise missiles to be placed on attack submarines. Others will be placed on B 52G bombers, entering full deployment in December 1982. The further forward plans are for 6,505 cruise missiles in the arsenal of the United States by 1989, of which 3,418 will be allocated to the Air Force and 2,527 to the Navy. No doubt most of these will be allocated to the European 'theatre'. Although the testing and production of ground-launched cruise missiles is now far behind schedule, the testing schedule of submarine-launched missiles is being pressed forward.

Already the 'New Jersey' and one other old battleship are being prepared as floating launchers, and batteries of up to 320 Tomahawk missiles could be placed on each. Thus on only two ships (one perhaps in the North Atlantic, the other in the Mediterranean) as many cruise missiles could be sited as have been planned for ground-launched missiles in all the five receiving NATO countries in Europe taken together.

Hence the peace movement–if it was to succeed in driving cruise missiles off European soil without also imposing a freeze upon these developments–would win only a Pyrrhic victory. And the Soviet military (if they accepted Reagan's zero option without the Ellsberg addition) would give up all their ground-launched intermediate missiles only to find themselves faced with a huge *additional* NATO arsenal on the waters off the continental shelf. It would be a very clever bit of NATO footwork: in one move, Soviet weapons would be reduced, NATO's would be enhanced, and Chancellor Schmidt's difficulties would go away.

But Reagan's zero option *plus* a freeze would close off that side-slip: it would close off also a number of monsters in preparation for us–the neutron bomb, the MX, Trident and whatever hissing of new SS's may be cooking at the other side. It would be an immense gain–a real turning-point for all the world. It would in one move clear out of Europe a whole nest of menacing intermediate weapons on both sides, and stabilise world-wide nuclear armaments preparatory to further negotiations.

Moreover, if Reagan is in earnest about START (Strategic Arms Reduction Talks) then a freeze now is a self-evident way in which to prepare for those negotiations.

There is one further reason why I commend Daniel Ellsberg's proposal. For a year a large part of the American peace movement has been campaigning for exactly such a freeze. They are mobilising growing support, in churches, on campuses, across the country. It is a proposal which makes good sense to Americans.

We have had difficulty, in the European peace movements, in coordinating our campaigns with theirs. A freeze makes sense for the superpowers; but here in Europe we have to get *rid* of weapons. To campaign in Europe for a freeze would be a step back from the campaign for a nuclear-free Europe, and also from the unilateralist demand for disarmament by direct initiatives by our own nations.

But if we put together the zero option (clearing a lot of intermediate weapons out of Europe) *with* the freeze, then the strategies of the European and American peace movements interlock. Together we could bring such pressure on the Geneva negotiations that we could carry our own proposals–those of the third force for peace–in the face of the objections of either side.

We need the help of the courageous and well-informed American peace movement. Europe may be forced to go it alone. But let us not understate the dangers. For this would make more unstable the existing instability of the Reagan administration and throw it back into its courses of aggressive isolationism, vainglorious militaristic theatre, and, perhaps, direct interventions in Central America and the Middle East. Only American citizens can resist these dangers. This is the time, not for easy anti-American rhetoric, but for strengthening the ties between ourselves and the other America.

That is why I commend the Ellsberg proposal to the attention of President Reagan, Mr Brezhnev, and to the consideration of the peace movement.

This is not 'the position' of the peace movement. Neither I nor Daniel Ellsberg have the right to pre-empt other voices. There will be many consultations. Better proposals may come forward.

Only large and clear proposals can command the support of the millions who have now demonstrated for peace in Europe's cities. These millions must hold firmly to their own zero option: *all* nuclear weapons out of Europe!

Our opponents talk about 'balance' and 'security'. There is no security in *any* missiles. The true security of Europe now lies in Europe's peace movements. If we become divided –and if we are divided from our American fellow workers– then our security will be at risk. Let the superpowers negotiate: but do not let them suppose that they have taken the argument from our hands and into theirs. Let them be aware, at every moment, of our voices and our demands encircling them from every side.

POLAND: A DEFEAT FOR PEACE

The long rolling Polish crisis was introducing 'instability'. Stability requires that the world of the East and the world of the West stay put, just as they are, for ever and anon, while both sides busy themselves with building up higher and more hideous 'defences', finding security in the 'strategic balance'.

As Professor Laurence Martin warned us in his third Reith Lecture, 'the Polish crisis is dangerous for NATO as well as the Warsaw pact'. For the retreat of Soviet hegemony in the East, which was dramatised by Solidarity, encouraged also the growth of neutralist and unilateralist sentiment in the West: it implicitly challenged United States hegemony at this side also.

That reassuring, settled structure, the Cold War, was beginning to lurch about, and the heavy ideological furniture was starting to slide around the floor on both sides.

Now it will be set back in place once more. We may relax, and go on hastening on cruise missiles and adding to the SS-20s comfortably, as before. Am I mistaken, or is there not only anguish but also an expression of relief in some corners of the house?

The Polish people were becoming ungovernable. The Polish economy was in a tailspin. Solidarity, so remarkable for its self-discipline in its early months, was becoming factional and intemperate, as a young generation—denied all experience of democratic practice—was flexing its muscles. What seemed possible was a re-enactment, on a huge and bloody scale, of Hungary 1956 or Prague 1968.

But—whatever this is—and I am writing on the fifth day

From *The Times*, 22 December 1981.

of the proclamation of martial law–it appears to be still a Polish solution. General Jaruzelski is a Polish patriot: he has pledged himself to avoid bloodshed. The Polish army is (or was?) perceived by the Polish people as a loyal servant of national interests. And the General has stated his intention of restoring normal political process (whatever normal can now mean in Poland) as soon as order is re-established.

These are commendable reasons for taking a measured view of the events of the first week of martial law–or at least for holding one's breath in hope. Yet this is certainly not the response of the general public, of every political persuasion. The spectacle of thousands of trade unionists being carted off to detention, of students being beaten up, of Polish Academicians being thrown into trucks, of tanks and troop carriers ringing steel works, mines and docks–this gives rise to uneasy memories. Wish as we may, we cannot believe that anything of the Polish renewal can survive even one week of martial law.

Insofar as I am an historian, it seems to me futile to predict the outcome of a military takeover from an assurance as to the good intentions of its prime movers. You cannot hang the outcome of an act of extreme social violence of this kind upon any man's intentions. In September 1980 the Turkish generals–no doubt honourable men also, and faced with very real disorders–imposed a 'temporary' martial rule. Now after fifteen months we are still reading of executions, internments, torture.

I would like to believe that General Jaruzelski's intentions are moderate and patriotic. I hope, in the face of all history's evidences, to wake up next week and learn that he has terminated martial law, and has handed power on to some National Council–of Solidarity, the Church, the Party, Academicians–which could steer the nation through emergency to further reform.

But Jaruzelski's intentions, however good, flew out of his heart and into the wintry night, at 3 a.m., when martial law was proclaimed and the first round-ups began. That night is now full of other persons' intentions: the intentions of other generals: of security police: of (perhaps) the young colonels in his shadow. And on Poland's frontiers there are other intentions pressing in upon the scene: the intentions of the military and security forces of 'fraternal' nations.

And against these inchoate intentions there will now be the intentions of resistance—of those who have been beaten, humiliated, herded into prison-camps without heating in the Baltic winter. There can be no way of erasing the acid-etched memories of these days, or of dispersing the sharp crystallisation of bitterly-opposed intentions as the consequences of force—and of resistance to force—unfold.

This is a major crisis of European political culture. We have only a week or two, and perhaps less, to press our own intentions also upon that desperate scene and to strive to influence its outcome.

By 'we' I mean all those forces, West or East, seeking for peaceful resolutions and for alternatives to the absolutes of Cold War ideologies: those forces which began to have influence in Europe in 1981—which glimpsed a possibility of putting the political culture of our continent back together once more.

I don't mean what has come to be called 'the peace movement' only. But Western European peace movements are a significant part of those forces. In my experience (of Scandinavia, Holland, West Germany and Britain) these movements have been drawn, in the main, from people in the liberal, trade unionist, Christian, democratic socialist and ecological traditions—people who have, in general, been active sympathisers with Solidarity—who sought to bring the cause of peace and the cause of freedom together.

The millions of people, many of them young, who have demonstrated for peace in Europe's capitals in the past two months have been informed by these sentiments. To describe them as 'pro-Soviet' or as 'orchestrated by Moscow' has always been a misrecognition. We have hoped that if we could relax the military and ideological pressure of the West upon the East, this would enlarge the space within which renewal might take place, in its own way, and at its own pace, on the other side.

Our strategy has only slowly met with a response from advocates of democratic rights in the East. At first it met with suspicion: was not this 'peace-loving' propaganda only designed to strengthen the diplomacy of the rulers of the Warsaw bloc?

If I were to criticise Solidarity (but criticisms and advice are now beside the point) it would be on this count. Too many of its leaders and advisers, and many of its young members, looked to the wrong friends in the West. They allowed Solidarity to be thrown as a joker into the weary Cold War card-game, in which the bluster of NATO spokesmen led always directly into the strong suit of the security-minded authorities of the other side.

Yet one needed only to look at a map. The way out for the Polish people could, and still can, only be along a different route. Only measures for relaxing the Cold War structures in Central Europe, and for the progressive demilitarisation of a Central European zone (perhaps taking in the two Germanys and Poland) on the lines of the old Rapacki Plan, could have afforded space for a very different (and democratic) kind of stabilisation. Only the common efforts of the Western peace movement (in its widest sense) and of Solidarity (and of 'liberals' in the Polish State) could have secured this space. This has been our argument.

And how could Solidarity, with its intense workaday preoccupations and its youthful, nationalistic forces, have set this strategy in motion? This is the most terrible reflection of all. It was not Solidarity but we, in the West, who ought to have taken the initiative to relax that tense epicentre of the confrontation of two blocs.

For Western governments have not just been spectators. They have been accomplices in that long and slow descent into martial law. The Western media have regarded 18 months of opening in Poland as a colourful spectacle: it offered all kinds of cues for Cold War theatricals. Instead of responding to the predicament of the Polish people, the leaders of NATO have been obsessed with their old antagonist, the Soviet leadership, and have directed one impotent threat after another at them, like Lear in his tantrums: 'I will have such revenges on you. . .'

> I will do such things–
> What they are, yet I know not; but they shall be
> The terrors of the earth. . .

Western governments have spent those long 18 months doing the arithmetic of the strategic balance, planning MX and Trident, forcing cruise missiles down the throats of the reluctant Western European public. There has been not one credible initiative from the West to the East—or directly to the insecure Polish government—offering to take the Rapacki Plan off the shelf or suggesting ways in which the military tension in Central Europe could be lessened.

This smug negativity and showy nuclear posturing was a factor beckoning on the declaration of martial law. Now there are three corpses left on the ground. The corpse of Solidarity. The corpse of Leninism, its last pretences of substituting for the working class blackened beyond recognition. And the corpse of NATO's professed concern for 'human rights'—the myth that human rights can be protected in the East by Western military menaces, or can be defended by empty threats of military revenges.

There has to be another way. This way is suggested in a statement which we have just received, by indirect routes, from friends in Prague. It was issued before the Polish events (on November 16th) by spokespersons of Charter 77, the courageous Czech centre of human rights supporters.

The statement links explicitly the two causes: peace and freedom. It is directly addressed to those elements (in my view the dominant elements) in the Western peace movement who also uphold the Helsinki agreement on human rights. The dependence of human rights and peace 'is mutual and works both ways'—

> It is hard to credit the sincerity of peace efforts by governments of countries in which people are persecuted for demanding that undertakings (made in the cause of detente) regarding human rights and fundamental freedoms be implemented. Similarly, it is difficult to regard as genuine champions of these rights and freedoms those who are stepping up the arms race and bringing close the danger of war.

'Our continent'—the statement continues—'faces the threat of being turned into a nuclear battlefield, into the burial-ground of its nations and of its civilisation which gave birth to the very concept of human rights.' And the statement concludes with a direct expression of solidarity with all those who work both for peace and for the Helsinki agreements: 'We do not have the opportunities they have to express as loudly our common conviction that peace and freedom are indivisible.'

The peace movement in the West must now make the indivisibility of these two causes even more explicit. Europe is threatened not only by missiles. It is threatened by the security and ideological structures which break our continent into two halves.

Martial law in Poland is not only an internal matter. The Western peace movement must make its own presence and intentions felt among those other pressures and intentions at work in the darkness over there. We, who *do* have the opportunities to express loudly our common conviction that 'peace and freedom are indivisible' must use our voices for our friends as well as for ourselves. We must let it be known to anyone over there with ears to hear that a defeat for freedom in Poland will be a devastating defeat also for peace.

COURTIER AT TOAD HALL

Professor Laurence Martin is not a pushy kind of fellow. He has crept up upon the British public by stealth. His publications are slender, but every paper has been placed judiciously and under prestigious auspices. He is 'an accepted figure in military circles' (we have been told in a *Times* profile) and has lectured to 140 NATO admirals, all in full uniform, in Norfolk, Virginia, drawing applause at the end. If the British public had not heard of him until last month it is because he is so self-effacing, and has been so busy interpreting our wishes over there in (the *Guardian*'s profile tells us) the 'world of strategic thinkers and generals and Pentagon heavies'.

Mr Martin is the soul of modesty. He would not wish us to be in too much awe of him as a heavy. Although he has come before us, on six occasions, as the BBC's Reith Lecturer, he is aware that there is little that he could do for us in such a limited time. 'I have devoted some of the brief time available to attacking some of the sacred cows of the less inhibited disarmers,' he noted in his final lecture. It seems clear that, if pushed a little, he might be willing to spare the time to attack them more.

But if he has attacked disarmers, he has the candour to add that he has done so 'not out of contempt but out of a due appreciation of their influence and importance'. It is reassuring to learn that one has not provoked the contempt of so distinguished and so authoritative a mind.

It was, without doubt, the ungraciousness of the BBC, in limiting Mr Martin to such a brief time, which prevented him from explaining *everything* to us. He simply was not afforded

---

This article first appeared in *New Society*, 24/31 December 1981.

space to analyse the evidence, nor to deploy new facts. Time and again he was forced to fall back upon mere assertion.

This is, perhaps, why even his most brilliant polemics fell short of conviction. Thus, in his first lecture, he smartly took out three of the sacred cows of disarmers in the space of three minutes. Observe his mode of attack.

The first cow was identified as the 'so-called "military-industrial complex", the alleged conspiracy of soldiers and armament manufacturers', who exaggerate the dangers of the antagonist in order to promote their 'own political and economic interests'.

Observe the marksmanship of 'so-called' and of 'alleged conspiracy'. That cow is desperately wounded by ridicule before even a shot has been fired. What moderate and balanced mind could possibly suppose that soldiers or arms manufacturers could conspire or have interests of their own? Not only is the 'military-industrial complex' laughed off the scene, but in the same moment General Eisenhower, Lord Zuckerman and a host of researchers are convicted of idiocy.

But a *coup de grace* is needed for this suffering cow. This is provided by reference to 'a recent, careful, statistical study of the subject', coming from Harvard, according to which tests for 'the presence of arms competition or arms racing' have proved negative. This is a finding of 'behavioural science'. It has been put in at one end of a computer and it has come out at the other end. It must be true.

Brilliant as this attack is, Mr Martin overlooked that he was faced here, not by one sacred cow, but by two. Hence his bullet went harmlessly in-between them both. For the notion of a military-industrial-complex, with its own inherent thrust and interests, and the metaphor of an arms race, whose thrust is derived from competition with the arms of an antagonist, are different and distinct.

Some recent studies have called in question the 'action-reaction' model, by which the upward growth in nuclear arms is the direct outcome of competition between the armourers of the two superpowers—that is, a 'race' in its usual sense. Attention has been redirected to inertial pressures on both sides—the long waves of R & D (research and development), 'technology creep', the imperatives of the 'alchemists' in the laboratories–which drive arms innovations forwards independently of any direct competition. (As a case in point, both the SS-20 and the cruise missile were developed independently of the other: it was never a case that one was a 'response' to the other, however convenient it may have been in subsequent propaganda to propose them as an equation.) And I would myself add to this the ideological drive of 'deterrence theory' itself, which, by continuously proposing worst-case scenarios as to possible developments on the other side, engenders new developments on its own side–and brings forward the worst-case scenario also.

The outcome of all this looks, in commonsense, like a 'race', but the competition between antagonists is indirect, and the mediations are so complex that they will evade Harvard's computer. This sacred cow–*both* cows–may safely graze in the lush pastures of the world's armaments a little longer.

But surely the *next* sacred cow is dead and ready for dinner? Disarmers are given to rabbitting on about the rising defence budget in the United States. Yet Mr Martin is able to show that the military share of the Federal budget *fell* from 49 per cent in 1960 to 23 per cent in 1981, and President Reagan is proposing only to put that up to 24 per cent in 1982. What a fuss and bother about 1 per cent, when in the long run the figures have been halved!

That bullet grazes the poor old cow: indeed, it may draw blood. Nuclear weapons may be hideously costly in their threat to life but they are not the most costly items in fiscal terms. Conventional weapons or launching platforms–aircraft carriers, submarines, tanks, bombers–are the major tax-eaters. An upwards growth in nuclear arms can co-exist with a downward drift in defence budgets.

Yet Mr Martin's aim was not as steady as might be supposed. He was too eager to make a showy killing. For a critical change in the procedures of US Federal budget accounting took place between 1965 and 1966. Before that time the US administration presented to Congress an 'administrative budget', of direct appropriations from the Treasury, which did not include 'trust funds'–i.e. Federal pensions and Social Security payments, some highway funds, and other moneys separately levied and paid out on the basis of recurrent authorising legislation.

But from 1966 these trust funds were included in one overall, greatly-enlarged, Federal budget: so that what had appeared before as 40 per cent for defence, re-appeared as 22 per cent of the newly-enlarged overall budget. It is the sort of magician's trick for which statistics, in agile hands, are a ready wand.

The Reith Lecturer will of course have been aware of this qualification (and it is a large one), and no doubt he would have explained it if the BBC had allowed him time. Meanwhile that sacred cow may bellow, but she will continue to graze.

The third sacred cow taken out is a notion of Mr George Kennan's that 'it has been we Americans, who, at almost every step of the road, have taken the lead in the development of this sort of weaponry'. This, Mr Martin observes sternly, 'is at best a half truth and the half that is true is not patently disgraceful'.

Mr Martin does not tell us why Mr Kennan's statement 'is at best a half truth'. What is half untrue about it? And if it is half untrue, why does Mr Martin then himself offer it to us, in his third lecture, as his own unqualified wisdom, when he refers to 'the traditional pattern in which each new technical sophistication has usually appeared first on the Western side'?

The notion that technical innovation might be 'disgraceful' is Mr Martin's and not Mr Kennan's. Mr Kennan had simply observed that the United States had led in every major innovation (from the first atomic bomb to thermonuclear weapons to MIRVs to cruise missiles), and had been pace-maker in what is now an insanely dangerous process.

But Mr Martin has already swivelled his rifle to take out Admiral Gene La Rocque, who is accused of giving aid and comfort to this same sacred cow. The Admiral's offence is to have invited Mr Martin to a conference in Groeningen last May on 'Nuclear War in Europe', with an accompanying letter deploring the new generation of nuclear weapons (which include cruise missiles and Pershing II) as 'more precise and more devastating'. 'Students of the subject,' avers Mr Martin, with the assumption of authority which befits a former Professor of War Studies (but not, it seems, a retired Admiral) 'will see an element of internal contradiction here: at least it all depends on what you don't want to devastate.' More precise weapons will destroy their targets with more accuracy, and there will be less devastation overall.

'A hit! A palpable hit!' And why is that sacred cow not bellowing and rolling on the ground? Professor Martin would have found out if he had been able to attend the Admiral's conference in Groeningen (I do not recall seeing him there) or had read the Admiral's own paper. For more accurate weapons can be more dangerous (if not necessarily more devastating) because they may encourage fantasies of the first strike at the opponent's silos (the Pershing II), or may be seen as instruments for nuclear war-fighting in more 'limited' or flexible ways. The old block-busting or city-burning theory of deterrence (MAD) fragments into a dozen scenarios of war-fighting at intermediate levels.

Admiral La Rocque (whose Center for Defense Information in Washington is well-informed) considers that the new, and more precise, weapons would make more probable the devastation of the 'theatre' of Europe. In his third lecture Mr Martin employed the device of caricature to scoff the notion aside: 'Some unilateralists, ably supported by several Soviet research institutes, suggest a positive American eagerness for a limited nuclear war confined to Europe.' Two minutes later, when his argument had taken a different turn, he referred—in an explanatory aside—to 'NATO's old plan of escalating to the theatre level, perhaps involving Soviet territory.' This sacred cow appears to be undeterred; but Mr Martin has shot off his own foot.

The lectures went on and on. Mr Martin was folksy and grave by turns. But since the BBC had allowed him so little time, he could spare little of it for facts and even less for arguments. He was reduced, of necessity, to presenting his prejudices and asserting his assertions, and in due course Messrs Weidenfeld will reproduce these (as they very often do) between hard covers.

If a lecturer has no original arguments to deploy, and is

reduced to mere assertion, then the problem becomes–how can *this* lecturer's assertions appear to be more wise, more authoritative, more judicious than any other's? The critic should attend less to the commonplaces that the lecturer uttered than to the strategy of his delivery.

This also was judiciously commonplace, but it deserves to be noted. I have marked my copy of the lectures with a series of yes-words and of no-words which are made to do the work which evidence or argument should have done.

The boo-words are what might be expected of a Defence Minister–let us say Mr John Nott–although not, perhaps, of a Reith Lecturer. In Lecture One disarmers are 'utopian , their attitudes made up of 'intellectual confusion, half-truths and downright error'; they are motivated by 'unreflective anti-militarism or gratuitous denigration of ourselves and our allies'; their impulses are 'dangerous', in some 'naive', in others 'disingenuous'.

In subsequent lectures such boo-words accumulate, and are compounded with a general pro-Soviet sneer. Opposition to cruise and Pershing missiles ('the Soviet campaign against the NATO decision') is presented as a Soviet intervention in 'the domestic European political debate'. The Soviet Union is given to 'intensive exploitation of well-meaning disarmament lobbies in the West'. Since the motives of these lobbies are suspect, and their intellectual equipment is derisory, their arguments clearly cannot trespass upon the brief time of our distinguished lecturer any further.

The yes-words are more numerous. They suggest academic retirement, prolonged and rigorous study, measured judgement. The arguments of opponents are always 'flawed'; his own assertions are the fruit of 'serious studies'. Asserting that 'the balance of power remains the best guiding principle for strategic policy', he adduces no new argument but falls back upon his own immense authority: 'I can only plead that after many years in strategic studies I have come to the conclusion that. . .'

For all his great modesty, Mr Martin allows us to know that he has been, over the years, privileged with the confidences of the Great. He introduces the names of his friends unobtrusively, without fuss: 'as Mr Dean Acheson once said to me'. Or thus:

> My friend, Albert Wohlstetter, the American strategist, the father of the phrase 'the delicate balance of terror'. . .

Mr Martin's privilege is, deftly, for a passing moment, conferred upon his auditors. How privileged we also are to be listening to an Authority who can number among his friends the father of so perspicacious and so illuminating a phrase!

It is Mr Martin's strategy also to claim always for his judgement less than his listeners would be ready to concede. His judgements (except where disarmers are concerned) are never strident. They are tentative. Sometimes, on questions as to which the rabble outside the studio has already snatched at 'easy and popular' remedies, the professor's own decision is refused.

If he must come down on one side rather than the other, it is always with reluctance: 'after some years of surveying the no-man's-land of strategic theory, I have yet to find a better hole than our present balance of power'. Even in the moment of decision, he grimaces at the loud Absolutes on every side of him. 'I do not rate myself very highly as a moralist,' he avers; or again, 'it would be presumptious and foolhardy for me to prescribe solutions.' 'In a climate where everybody seems to be pushing some cheap or easy remedy a note of caution may not come amiss.'

How admirable this modesty, and how judicious these repeated evasions of open judgements! And if so high an Authority as Mr Martin, with his long and arduous years in strategic studies, confesses that it would be 'presumptuous' in him to suggest solutions, how much more incapable we, his unlettered listeners, must be! How brash it is for CND to mill around the streets in its 'easy and popular' way!

Mr Martin's strategy is to put two old tricks together: the arched eyebrow of the academy, raised in disdain and rigour, and the inside know-how of the expert, privy to the confidences of the Establishment. He has listened all these years to the dramas of the Great, like Polonius behind the arras. And he chooses just those terms which Polonius, if he had been elevated to a Chair of War Studies instead of being brutally cut short by the blade of a confused disarmer, would have used to decorate his inaugural lecture: 'symmetry', 'appropriateness', 'credible', 'legitimacy', 'modest but intensely practical approaches'.

He wishes it to be supposed that he is offering nothing in the least unusual: 'I must confess at the outset that I, at least, have no such complete assurance about the prescriptions that are, on balance, the best I can discover.' He wishes to be taken as just one other in the long line of Reith lecturers: the bland leading the bland.

The Reith Lectureship is an *ad hominem* appointment. 'They', or someone up there, decides who is an 'expert', and confers this distinction upon their choice. It is inevitable that we should examine these credentials in our turn, and submit the incumbent to our own *ad hominem* scrutiny.

Yet I cannot be content with a notion of Mr Martin as Professor Polonius or Professor Pangloss. There is something else to him than that. For his strategy of lecturing was too evident: it was a device, not only for imposing his opinions upon the audience, but also for concealing their true character. There is something more to Professor Martin than 'realism' and 'moderation'.

He has, after all, climbed upwards inexorably, yet it would seem from the newspaper profiles that he has found advancement always by stealth, on an inside track, hidden from public view. His biographers say something about the positions he has held, but little to indicate any intellectual achievement. He has acquired the hubris of the academic, but without acquitting himself in any recognised academic discipline. Indeed, although he is a leading practitioner of strategic studies he 'freely expresses doubts' (*The Times* informs us) 'about whether it should be an academic discipline at all.'

These doubts are well-founded. Strategic studies, if they are not admixed with a reputable discipline–of the economist, the political theorist, or the historian–are a no-discipline. They are the apologetics of military power. They commence with militarist assumptions–as to the virtues of 'deterrence' and the 'balance of terror'—and after long and tedious years of consultancies and conferences around the globe, the very same assumptions are recycled with authority as Reith Lectures. The only change is that the 'balance' which must now be maintained is at a higher and more sophisticated level.

Mr Martin is a new kind of intellectual creature. He has prospered as a courtier to the nuclear weapons systems and their Defence establishments. A courtier to them he is also a courier to us—it is his business to convey to us their imperatives:

> If you speak to the technicians at the nuclear laboratories, you learn that it is not as simple as it looks. The case for Trident appears in a stronger light when you talk to the experts.

He has been employed (he has told the *Guardian*) as a courier on even nicer and more secret matters. It was through him that the Pentagon sent a message to 'the Brits' that it would facilitate the 'Chevaline' modernisation programme to the Polaris warhead. The 'Brits' who were then informed did not include the British public, nor even the British Cabinet. A courtier, like a courtesan, must know the value of privacy.

Mr Martin's biographers give little away. He went up to Cambridge in 1945, when World War II had just ended. He did some service in the peacetime RAF. Went on to Yale, to MIT, was a consultant at the NATO defence college and to the Los Alamos weapons laboratories. At Yale he ran a radio show called 'Religion at the Newsdesk', but without unseemly fervour: 'I go to church occasionally. I am not an unreligious man.'

He is a great conference-goer, consorting with Dr Kissinger and Caspar Weinberger at Williamsburg, or in the more secret events of the European-American Institute for Security Studies ('he hints at the Institute's value in keeping Turkey loyal to NATO'). And all of this, which might weigh heavily on some, he has taken lightly, in the best tradition of the English intellectual dilettante. The Vice-Chancellorship of Newcastle University, which he was gracious enough to accept in 1978, 'he regards in some ways as his first real job'.

Lesser men might have supposed that his previous post, as Professor of War Studies at King's College, London, was a 'real job'. There have been wars enough to study.

He is a new kind of Mid-Atlantic creature, whose formative intellectual experiences must have been laid down in that traumatic Mid-Atlantic moment, the genesis of the Cold War. His biographers provide only two clues to this formation. Mr Martin is devoted to *Wind in the Willows.* One may suppose a certain transference of that childhood affection into a myth underlying all his 'strategic studies': the friendly, anthropomorphic creatures of NATO–Mole, Badger, Ratty and even the Transatlantic Toad–threatened at every step by the wild creatures of the Soviet woods.

The other clue comes from *The Times.* Mr Martin went up to Cambridge in 1945, at the age of 17, 'and all his contemporaries were 35 with the Military Cross.' It gave him, he concedes, 'a certain respect for the military'. But something here has been mis-remembered, and has been skewed into myth. Some of Mr Martin's contemporaries at Cambridge then (of whom I was one) had returned from the services or from other kinds of 'war work': few of them were 35, fewer had the Military Cross, a good number of them were women, and if we shared anything in common it was *dis*respect for the military and delight at shedding that transient disguise.

Mr Martin's misrecognition of the situation took my mind back to Isherwood's *Lions and Shadows*–an autobiography of a youth at Cambridge immediately after World War I.

> Like most of my generation I was obsessed by a complex of terrors and longings connected with the idea 'War'. 'War', in this purely neurotic sense, meant The Test. The Test of your courage, of your maturity, of your sexual prowess: 'Are you really a Man?'

How abrupt the mutations of generations, the shifts in cultural cohorts may be! As my 'generation' was just shaking 'War' off ourselves, as a dog shakes water off its coat, Mr Martin's generation (some four or five years our juniors) was obsessed by the war they had just missed: the Test. Can this obsession have carried him through all these years, all that transatlantic conferring, to the Chair of War Studies and, at last, to the imperial purple of Reith?

Mr Martin has proposed a problem to his own vaulting ambition. There is scarcely anywhere where he can now go, after these distinguished lectures, save into the House of Lords.

If I might offer him a small service, I would propose to him a title, appropriate to the courtier of deterrence: Lord Prufrock of Los Alamos:

> . . . an attendant lord, one that will do
> To swell a progress, start a scene or two,
> Advise the prince; no doubt, an easy tool,
> Deferential, glad to be of use,
> Politic, cautious, and meticulous;
> Full of high sentence, but a bit obtuse;
> At times, indeed almost ridiculous–
> Almost, at times, the Fool.

I propose the title. But now I must take it back. For if we allow him this, then he has succeeded in his imposture. It was his strategy to come forward thus; to pretend to offer a courtier's homiletics: to confirm the bigoted in the good repute of their bigotry: to reassure the anxious with platitudes: and to leave his opponents with nothing to throw back save grimaces and names–'Yah! Prufrock, Pangloss, Polonius!' The strategy was to come before us as a 'moderate', and make all other views appear as utopian or extreme.

Yet it is Professor Martin who is an extremist. He advocates some of the most extreme views which it is possible for anyone in our time to hold. He approves of every deadly weapons-system which now exists, and he approves of their continuing innovation.

As I run through these lectures and separate the true *import* from its several disguises I find these judgements. The Polaris submarine is 'a valuable contribution to several forms of strategic stability'. General disarmament is undesirable, and would be impossible to verify. The introduction of cruise and Pershing II missiles may not be 'essential' but may well be prudent as part of the 'refurbishment' of 'the whole

Western nuclear arsenal'. NATO must continue to reserve to itself the right of first nuclear use. Nuclear proliferation may be good or bad: a Libyan bomb would be 'a *terrifying* thought' but an Israeli one may be a comforting one: 'nevertheless. . . I think the burden of proof is on anyone who wants to encourage a new power to join the nuclear ranks'. The arms trade is 'much denigrated', since it may play 'an essential role in curbing proliferation' (the superpowers can buy the Third World off with tanks and bombers instead). A Rapid Deployment Force (it is implied, in Lecture Four) is urgent and desirable, and European nations–in particular Britain and France–should make more contribution outside Europe. A complete test ban would be bad. Arms control may be permitted, in certain conditions, but it is undesirable to let it be supposed that it can result in *dis*armament. Although 'not fully qualified to judge' the merits of Trident, Professor Martin is in favour of it.

If we do not conclude that these views, taken together, are nihilist and extremist, then we must conclude that the course of civilisation is already run. This is, perhaps, Mr Martin's own conclusion–and the assumption from which he started out.

The first line of Lecture One is this: 'Armed force is the ultimate tool of political conflict.' The sentence is intended to echo Clausewitz: but we have come a long way from that old philosopher. War may be the continuation of politics by other means, but the means are *other* than the means of politics. To suggest that armed force is 'the ultimate tool' of politics is to suggest that it is normal, or at least inevitable. Murder may be the continuation of a marital dispute by other means, but we might hesitate before we concluded that murder is 'the ultimate tool' of marital relations. It is the business of civilisation to refuse the means of war just as we refuse the means of murder. Mr Martin, who has other business, regards warfare as normal and peace 'as a kind of suspended war'.

I find these extremist views objectionable. I find it objectionable to refer to the Soviet Union as 'the enemy'. And I find even more objectionable (and disturbing as I write these lines) some views propounded (with moderation) in

Lecture Three. The Polish crisis, Mr Martin argues, 'is dangerous for NATO as well as the Warsaw pact.' And why is this? The Poles have been immoderate; they have upset stability.

Professor Martin is concerned, of course, only with 'strategic implications'. 'It is not my place', he reassures us, to explore 'political possibilities.' But in a disinterested *strategic* view it can be seen that 'previous episodes–Hungary, Czechoslovakia, Afghanistan' did nothing to the strategic balance but good. They made NATO 'more lively in its military preparations'. There were more conferences to give papers to, more consulting to do at Los Alamos.

But, gracious heavens, the danger of this episode was that the Poles might have *succeeded!* The Soviet hegemony might have been rolled back. And this would have encouraged 'neutralists and unilateralists' in the West to roll back United States military power as well. This could erode 'European contributions to NATO' and this conjoint prospect, of the Cold War actually *receding* in both halves of Europe, Mr Martin 'would find highly alarming'.

No doubt he finds the latest news from Poland to be reassuring. The Cold War will go on. NATO will become 'more lively' once again. As my own vision of the astonishing opportunities of this year, 1981, when we might have begun to put Europe back together, begins to close, Mr Martin's perspectives open once again.

And yet, in this moment of closure and of opening, the terrifying configurations of Professor Martin's form of extremism are suddenly apparent. For he is not, after all, concerned with a discipline within its own compartment:. a discrete aspect of human life: strategic studies. He is claiming the *whole* of life. For we glimpse at last that 'the strategic balance' is an on-going social and economic system in itself, to which all other aspects of our lives are now subordinate. Like some gigantic, expanding ectoplasm 'the strategic balance' of nuclear weaponry hangs above us, sucking up everything–our taxes, our hopes, the last outposts of Gaelic culture, the aspirations of the Polish or Greek peoples–into itself. We may do no more than creep (with moderation) beneath it, serving its voracious appetite, keeping the system adjusted. Eventually, we know, it will suck in the ecosphere itself.

And now at last I can see who Professor Martin is. He is an Alien, descended from that alienated ectoplasmic world, to instruct us in our duties to The System. The Reith Lectures were a Close Encounter of the Fourth Kind. If we are dutiful, moderate and prudent, we may expect a Fifth Kind of Encounter. It will be the last.

BEYOND THE COLD WAR

I am honoured to have been invited to deliver this lecture, here in my own city, by a committee of fellow-citizens of no particular political persuasion, united by their concern for serious and open discussion. It is kind of you to open the Guildhall to me, and to make me so much at home.

My difficulty is that I have been favoured with so much publicity for a lecture which I did *not* deliver that any lecture which I do now deliver is bound to come as an anti-climax. It is as if the bishops were finally to assemble and open Joanna Southcott's mysterious box, and find nothing within it but a recipe for making muffins.

And yet I can glimpse, out of the corner of my eye, something which may be important. I wish I could see it more clearly, and describe it clearly to you. I think that we may now be living, this year and for several years ahead, through episodes as significant as any known in the human record.

I will not dwell on the perils. We are well aware of these. Human ingenuity has somehow created these immense destructive powers, which now appear to hang above us, alienated from all human control. They are now talking of siting laser weapons on the moon—weapons which, in a literal sense, will be lunatic.

We are aware, all of us, of the overplus of this nuclear weaponry, much of it crammed into our own continent: land-mines, artillery, torpedoes, depth-charges, missiles launched from the ground, from submarines, from the air. We may differ as to the exact 'balance' of weaponry held by the adversary parties. But we are also aware that, when the

---

This is the text of what had originally been intended as the Dimbleby Lecture, 1981. Owing to the withdrawal of the BBC's invitation, it was delivered in Worcester on 26 November 1981.

overkill capacity of weaponry is such as to enable the destruction of civilised conditions for life on our continent thirty times over, calculations of 'balance' are becoming irrelevant.

We may also, after two years of mounting anxiety, begin to feel slight twinges of hope. The superpowers have at last been brought to the negotiating table. Something might even be done to halt or to reduce the weaponry in Europe.

This is good. But what an effort it has taken to get the politicians there! And what a discrepancy there is between the procedures of war and those of peace! The decisions to develop new weapons—to deploy the SS-20, to put the neutron bomb into production, to go ahead with cruise missiles—are taken by a few score people—at the most by a few hundred—secretively, behind closed doors, on both sides. But to check, or to reverse, any one of those decisions, nothing will do except the voluntary efforts of hundreds of thousands—late into the night and through weekends, month after month—addressing envelopes, collating information, raising money, meeting in churches or in school halls, debating in conferences, lobbying parliaments, marching through the streets of Europe's capital cities.

In the past 18 months I have visited fellow workers for peace in the United States, in Czechoslovakia, in Finland, Norway, Denmark, Belgium, Holland, Germany and France. The story is always the same. People are determined. They are encouraged by growing support. But they are running out of puff. How long can they go on?

And if they relax, then in two or three years the weapons—accompanied by new weapons of equal barbarity, nerve-gas, bacteriological warfare—will begin to come back. We are running the wrong way down an escalator: if we stop running we will be carried up to the top.

To check the missiles is something. But the political launch-pad for all these missiles is the adversary posture of the two great rival alliances, grouped around the USA and USSR: that is, the Cold War. If this adversary posture were to be modified—if it were to be undermined by new ideas and movements on *both* sides—then, not only the weapons, but the launch-pad for them would be taken away. And many of the difficulties attending disarmament, whether nuclear or conventional, would fall also.

This is what I shall examine in this lecture. I do not intend to rehearse the history of the Cold War, nor to examine, once again, why it started. I will enquire into its real content *today*. What is the Cold War now about? Is it necessary? And, if it is, whose is the need?

Let us go back, first, not to the origin of the Cold War, but to a moment just before it broke out. My own generation is the last which witnessed that moment as adults. Our perception of 'Europe' remains, to this day, a little different from that of younger generations. Europe, for us, included Warsaw, Prague and Budapest and, more distantly, Leningrad and Moscow. But for many young Westerners, 'Europe' now means, first of all, the EEC.

The young have grown up within a fractured continent. The Cold War has been a received condition, which has set the first premises of politics and ideology from before the time of their birth. It is now a settled and unquestioned premise: a habit. Most people assume that the condition will persist—far into the 21st century, for the full length of their own lifetimes—if war does not supervene. It has always been there.

But it has not always been there. I do not suggest that Europe, before the Cold War, was in any way, politically or culturally, united. It was the seat of rival imperialisms which extended over the globe. It was the seat and source of two devastating world wars. It was a battlefield for opposing ideologies.

Yet the savage divisions among Europeans did not exist as a fracture splitting the continent in half. They ran deeply *within* the political and cultural life of each nation-state. European states went to war; yet Europeans remained within a common political discourse.

This was true, most of all, in the climactic years of the second world war. From 1941 to 1944 Nazi Germany and its allies occupied an area and commanded resources very much greater than the EEC. Yet, paradoxically, there grew up within occupied Europe a new internationalism of common resistance.

From Norway to Montenegro, from the coast of Kent to the suburbs of Stalingrad—and it is necessary to recall, with an effort, that Britain and Russia then were allies and that it was the prodigious sacrifice of Soviet life which turned the tide of that war—there was a common movement of resistance. Polish and Czech units served alongside British forces; British liaison groups—among them Churchill's son, Randolph, and the Conservative MP, Brigadier Fitzroy Maclean—served with the Yugoslav partisans.

It is the fashion to be cynical about all that now, and for good reasons. The expectations and hopes of that moment were naive. The alliance of anti-fascist resistance—the alliances of liberals, Communists, agrarians, social-democrats, Conservatives—were later dishonoured, and on both sides.

But we might also recall that they were honoured for a while, and honoured with sacrifice of life. The aspiration for a democratic Europe—extending the good faith of those alliances forward into the peace—was authentic.

Some of these expectations were to be betrayed. But they remain there, in the record. I have said that others now seem to us as naive. Here is a young British officer—aged twenty-two—writing in a private letter from the Middle-East in 1943:

> How wonderful it would be to call Europe one's fatherland, and think of Krakow, Munich, Rome, Arles, Madrid as one's own cities. I am not yet educated to a broader nationalism, but for a United States of Europe I could feel a patriotism far transcending my love for England.

This Union he saw as 'the only alternative to disaster'. And later in the same year he wrote:

> There is a spirit abroad in Europe which is finer and braver than anything that tired continent has known for centuries, and which cannot be withstood. You can, if you like, think of it in terms of politics, but it is broader and more generous than any dogma. It is the confident will of whole peoples, who have known the utmost humiliation and suffering and have triumphed over it, to build their own lives once and for all. . . There is a marvellous opportunity before us—and all that is required from Britain, America and the USSR is imagination, help and sympathy. . .

What sad reading this makes today! Some will find it Euro-centric, others will find it sentimental or innocent in its view of the motives of politicians and states, all will know that the hopes were to be defeated, within two or three years, by events. But the expectations were commitments, to the extent of life itself, and they were shared by many thousands across the continent.

In January 1944 this officer wrote to his brother:

> My eyes fill very quickly with tears when I think what a splendid Europe we shall build (I say Europe because that's the only continent I really know quite well) when all the vitality and talent of its indomitable peoples can be set free for co-operation and creation.

Ten days later he parachuted onto a high plateau in East Serbia—in the region of Tsrna Trava—where he was to serve as liaison officer with a contingent of Bulgarian partisans.

It is not my business now to record the savage warfare and the privations of the next months, as these partisans and their small British support-group were driven backwards and forwards across the snow-fields by superior forces. It is a complex story, clouded by the refusal of the British authorities, to this day, to release some archives. In May small Bulgarian partisan forces set off on an ill-planned and ill-fated drive directly into the heart of Bulgaria. They were overwhelmed; most of them were massacred; and the British officer, my brother, was executed. He was subsequently proclaimed a National Hero of Bulgaria, and despite some nasty twists and turns in Bulgarian politics, he remains that to this day. I have been, twice, along the route of that march; my wife and I two years ago visited the mountains around Tsrna Trava and talked with surviving partisans. The events of that time have not been forgotten, although they have been clouded by Cold War mythology, and on both sides. But that, again, is a different and complex story.

My point is this. My brother's aspirations for the future were not unusual, although his fate exemplified the cause of this common resistance in an unusual way. Throughout Europe men and women looked forward to the fruits of victory: a continent both democratic and at peace. There would be different social systems, of course. But it was supposed that these systems would be chosen by each nation, with popular consent. The differences need not be occasions of war.

These expectations were becoming casualties when British forces confronted Greek partisans in Athens in December 1944. None survived the shock of the onset of the Cold War. The polarisation was absolute. I am not concerned, now, to examine why this happened. But happen it certainly did. Communists were expelled from the political life of the West: in France, in Italy, and to the prison islands of Greece. Liberals, social-democrats, agrarians, and, then, Communists who had proved to be too sympathetic to the alliance with democracy or too critical of Stalin: all these were purged from the political life of the East. Some were subjected to monstrous faked trials, were executed or imprisoned. The Cold War era, of two hostile Europes, commenced.

I will make only one, over-simplified, comment on that moment. The cause of freedom and the cause of peace seemed to break apart. The 'West' claimed freedom; the 'East' claimed the cause of peace. One might talk for hour upon hour in qualification of both claims. Each is made up of one part of truth and another part of hypocrisy. 'The West', whether directly through NATO or indirectly through the arrangements of the United States military, co-existed and co-exists easily enough with regimes notorious for their abuse of freedom and of human rights: with Salazar's Portugal, Franco's Spain, the Greece of the Colonels, or with the military tyranny in Turkey today. And this is before we look to Latin America, Asia or Africa. The Soviet Union's dedication to 'peace' co-existed with the military repression of unacceptable motions towards democracy or autonomy within its client states: notoriously in Hungary, 1956, and Czechoslovakia, 1968. And this is before we look towards the military support given to Third World regimes within the Soviet sphere of influence, or towards Afghanistan.

But, in the time open to me, I can only note both claims, which have long underpinned the ideological contestations of the Cold War. And I must add that, when every allowance is made for hypocrisy, both claims have a little colour. It is not that 'the Free West' has been an exemplar of democratic practice. But it is in the West that certain important democratic practices have persisted, whereas in 'the East'—after *gulag* and faked trial, the repression of the Hungarian insurrection and of the Prague Spring, the psychiatric confinement of dissidents, and the monotonous State-licensed idiocy of Communist intellectual orthodoxy—the very term 'People's Democracy' became sick.

That is familiar, and a source of much self-congratulation to Westerners. What is less familiar—for the young are not taught this carefully in our schools—is that the West was perceived by the East—and perceived for good reasons—as the most threatening and irresponsible military power. The first atomic detonation over Hiroshima, by the United States (but with the assent of our own government) sent panic-waves across the Communist world which contributed much to the onset of Cold War. From that moment, and for over twenty years, there was no question of 'balance' in the nuclear arsenals of the two parties: the West had an overwhelming superiority in destructive nuclear power.

We have been reminded of this recently by two independent voices of authority, each of them dissenting voices from the opposed superpowers. George Kennan, the former American ambassador to Moscow whose famous despatch (by 'Mr. X' in *Foreign Affairs,* July 1947) contributed to the post-war policies of United States' 'containment' of the Soviet Union, has reminded Americans that 'it has been we. . . who, at almost every step of the road, have taken the lead in the development of this sort of weaponry.' (This is not, by the way, as the BBC Reith Lecturer for 1981 has alleged in his know-all way, 'at best a half truth': it is a plain, and easily verifiable, fact). And Roy Medvedev, the Soviet supporter of free intellectual enquiry and civil rights, has commented that, with the brief exception of the Soviet advance in satellite technology in 1957-8, the United States has always led in weapons technology—

> obliging the USSR to try to catch up from a position of inferiority. This permanent dynamic has structured Russian responses deeply, creating a pervasive inferiority complex that has probably prevailed over rational calculations in the 70s.

It is a dramatic instance of the trajectory of our times that these two distinguished men, starting from such different presuppositions and passing through such differing experiences, should have now come to a common point of commitment in support for the active peace movement.

From August 1945 onwards there were voices enough to argue that 'the West' should put its advantage in nuclear weapons technology to use. These voices went on for many years—calling for a 'preventive war' or for the 'liberation' of Berlin or of East Europe. Some voices were influential enough—John Foster Dulles, James Forrestal (the paranoid United States Secretary for the Navy who went mad in office)—to induce a legitimate 'paranoia' on the other side. The United States has rattled its nuclear weapons in their scabbard, as a matter of state policy, on at least 19 occasions. By the end of the 1940s it had surrounded the Soviet Union with a ring of forward strategic air-bases, all—with the exception of Alaska—outside United States' territory. The only attempt by the Soviet Union to establish a comparable forward base was repelled by the direct ultimatum of nuclear attack: the Cuban missile crisis. The humiliation suffered then by the Soviet rulers powered the upward build-up of Soviet missiles in the 1960s.

I am not endorsing either claim without qualification. I mean only to repeat that both claims had colour: the West to 'freedom' and the East to 'peace'. And this placed the political culture of Europe in a permanent double-bind. Those who worked for freedom in the East were suspected or exposed as agents of Western imperialism. Those who worked for peace in the West were suspected or exposed as pro-Soviet 'fellow travellers' or dupes of the Kremlin. In this way the rival ideologies of the Cold War disarmed those, on both sides, who might have put Europe back together. Any transcontinental movement for peace *and* freedom became impossible. Such a movement glowed for a moment in 1956 and, again, in 1968. Each time it was, ironically, the 'peace-loving' Soviet forces which ground out the sparks under an armoured heel.

Let us move back to our own time. For I am addressing the

question—not what caused the Cold War, but what is it about today? And it is no good trying to answer this by standing at its source and stirring it about with a stick. For a river gathers up many tributaries on its way, and turns into unexpected courses.

Nor is it any good asking me to deliver to you some homilies called 'the lessons of history'. History teaches no simple lessons, because it *never* repeats itself, even if certain large themes recur.

In fact, received notions of the 'lessons' of recent history are often actively unhelpful in dealing with the present, since these establish stereotypes which interfere with contemporary vision. This is very much the case with today's Cold War. Because it was widely believed in the 1930s that World War I was 'caused' by an arms race and by inflexible structures of alliances, essential measures of collective security were not taken to halt Hitler and to prevent World War II. Today the 'lesson' of World War II has stuck in the public mind while the 'lesson' of World War I has been forgotten. Because it is widely believed that military weakness and appeasement 'caused' World War II, many people now condone new forms of militarisation which will, if unchecked, give us World War III.

At the same time there is, in both West and East, a simple transference of remembered images to the present. The 1930s burned in memory the image of a major militarist and expansionist power (Nazi Germany) whose appetite was only fed by each new scrap of appeasement; which had an insatiable drive to conquer all Europe, if not the world. Politicians and ideologists, West and East, have renamed this insatiable potential aggressor as (respectively) Russia or America. It is a compelling identification. Yet it rests on the assent of memory rather than upon analysis or evidence. It appears plausible simply because it looks so familiar.

But to understand the present we must first resist the great suggestive-power of memory. This is, surprisingly, where the historical discipline may be helpful, may teach 'lessons' of a different kind. For historians deal always with long-term eventuations—social, political, economic process—which continually defeat or contradict the expectations of the leading historical actors themselves.

History never happens as the actors plan or expect. It is the record of *unintended* consequences. Revolutions are made, manifestos are issued, battles are won: but the outcome, twenty or thirty years on, is always something that no-one willed and no-one expected. Boris Pasternak, the great Russian poet, reflected in *Dr Zhivago* on the 'indirect results' of the October Revolution, which 'have begun to make themselves felt–the fruits of fruits, the consequences of consequences.'

I like this phrase, 'the consequences of consequences', and wish we could see the Cold War in this way and not in terms of the intentions of the actors in 1947. We might see it, then, more clearly, as an abnormal political condition. It was the product of particular contingencies at the end of World War II which struck the flowing rivers of political culture into glaciated stasis, and struck intellectual culture with an ideological permafrost. The Cold War frontiers were fixed, in some part, precisely by 'deterrence'–by the unprecedented destructive power of the nuclear weaponry which, by coincidence, was invented at this historical moment.

It is an odd and very dangerous condition. A line has been drawn across the whole continent, like some gigantic geological fault, with one great capital city catapulted across the fault and divided internally by a wall. On each side of this line there are not only vast accumulations of weaponry directed against the other, but also hostile ideologies, security operations, and political structures. Both sides are preparing, and over-preparing, for a war in which both would share in mutual ruin. Yet both parties deny any intention of attacking the other: both mutter on about 'deterrence' or 'defence.'

If we ask the partisans of either side what the Cold War is now about, they regard us with the glazed eyes of addicts. It is there because it is there. It is there (they might say) because of the irreconcilable antagonism between two political and social systems: totalitarianism versus democracy–or Communism versus capitalism or Western imperialism. Each must be motivated, of its own inherent nature, by the desire to vanquish the other. Only the mutual fear of ‘deterrence’ can stave off a total confrontation.

The trouble with these answers is that they are phrased in terms of the ideological justifications for the Cold War at the moment of its origin. They remain fixed, in the perma-frost of that icy moment.

A brief survey will show us that the notion of two mono-lithic adversary systems conforms uneasily with the evidence of the past decades. To take the Communist bloc first: if it is aiming to vanquish Europe and then the World, it is making a bad job of it. It has lost Yugoslavia. It has lost Albania. The Soviet Union and China have split bitterly apart. From the time of the post-war settlement, which established a protect-ive belt of client Communist states around Russia’s western frontiers, there has been no further expansion into European territory. Twenty-five years ago Soviet and NATO forces were withdrawn from Austria, and the peace treaty which guaranteed Austria’s neutrality has been honoured by both sides.

There has also been a major recession in pro-Soviet Communist movements in the West. The Cominform, established in 1947, was seen by Western ideologists as a Trojan horse within Western societies: or a whole set of Trojan horses, the largest being in Italy and France. The Cominform has long been broken up. Disgusted by the events of 1956, by the Soviet repression of the ‘Prague Spring’ in 1968, most Western parties have turned in a ‘Eurocommunist’ direction: they are sharply critical of the Soviet denial of civil rights, oppose Soviet military policies (including the intervention in Afghanistan), and in general have supported Polish Solidarity. This is true of the huge Italian Communist Party (which endorses a critical commit-ment to NATO), of the influential Spanish party, and of the small British party. The French Communist Party, which has been ambiguous on questions of civil rights has steadily lost support in the French electorate.

Or take the question of Marxism. In Cold War fiction Soviet Communism is supposed to be motivated by a philosophy, ‘Godless Marxism’, with universal claims. The strange development here is, not only that religion appears to be reviving in most parts of the Communist world, but that the intellectual universe of Marxism is now in chaos. In the Warsaw Pact countries there is something called Marxism-Leninism, learned by rote, which is a necessary rhetoric for those who wish to advance within the career structures of the state. It provokes, in the public generally, nothing but a yawn. I can think of no Soviet intellectual who, *as a Marxist,* commands any intellectual authority outside the Soviet Union.

Yet, in an odd sideways movement, Marxism as an intellectual system has migrated to the West and to the Third World, just as certain liberal beliefs have been migrating to dissident circles in the Communist world. Marxism in the West has fragmented into a hundred argumentative schools. And most of these schools are profoundly critical of the Soviet Union and of Communist practice. Marxism is certainly a vigorous intellectual influence in the West and in the Third World—an influence at work in many universities, journals, and works of scholarship. But whatever this Marxism may be—and it is becoming difficult to say what it is—it has nothing whatsoever to do with Soviet expansionism.

Look where we will, the evidence is at odds with the Cold War fictions. Poland is only one of several East European nations which are now deeply indebted to Western banks. What are we to make of a 'people's democracy' in hock to the capitalists? The Soviet Union depends for grain upon the prairies of the Mid-West of America, and the farmers of the Mid-West depend, in turn, upon these annual sales. West Germany has recently completed an agreement which will bring natural gas from Siberia, to the extent of close on 10 per cent of the country's energy needs. The French government is at present negotiating a similar agreement for natural gas which 'would make France depend on Soviet gas for 26 per cent of its requirements in 1990 (*Times*, 11 November 1981). Long-standing trade agreements traverse both blocs and there is even that phenomenon, which one observer has described as 'vodka-cola', by which Western multinationals have invested in Soviet and East European enterprises, taking advantage of the low labour costs and the absence of industrial conflict in the Communist world. Even the Soviet ICBMs may incorporate components of United States design or manufacture. Of course the American military reserve the top-flight computers and technology for their own use. I do not know whether the American public should draw comfort from the fact that the ICBMs directed at them may be guided by second-rate components of their own design.

I am not saying that the social and political systems of East and West are identical or even comparable. I am saying that the first Cold War premise–of irreconcilable adversary posture between the blocs across the whole board–has become a fiction. And in the course of last year, events in Poland have made the old fiction look even odder. We now have a Polish pope. We also have a huge, nationalist and Catholic, but also socialist, Polish trade union movement, Solidarity, a great deal more insurgent, and more far-reaching in its demands, than any union movement in the West. To be sure, the Russians do not like this at all. But they have not, as yet, been able to stop it, and the longer it succeeds the more its example is likely to prove contagious. Once again, if we assume that the aim of Soviet Communism is to overrun all Europe, then it is not doing very well. It can't even hold what it has.

If we turn the picture around, and look at the West, we discover other contradictions. At the moment of the Cold War's origin–when the permafrost set in–the United States had emerged from the Second World War, alone of all the advanced economies, with a huge unimpaired productive capacity. The 'American Century' was, exactly, *then:* economic and military strength were overwhelming, and diplomatic and cultural influence ensued. NATO, perforce, was an alliance expressive of United States hegemony, and, in its military structure, under direct American command.

But the American Century was not to last for a hundred years. In past decades the American economy has entered into a long secular decline in relation to its competitors: Japan, the EEC powers (notably West Germany and France). The cultural influence and the diplomatic authority of the United States has entered a similar decline. And United States conventional military forces also suffered a catastrophic defeat in Vietnam. Only the overwhelming nuclear strength has been maintained–has grown year after year–has been protracted beyond the moment of its origin. United States militarism seeks to extend forward indefinitely—to cast its shadow across Europe—a supremacy of economic and political force which existed thirty years ago but which has long ceased to exist. In one sense the present crisis in Western Europe can be read in this way. The United States is seeking to use the muscle of its nuclear weaponry to compensate for its loss of real influence.

This crisis has been reflected first, and most sharply, within Western European Social-Democratic and Labour movements. When the Cold War first struck, there was a fierce contest within these movements. This was (I must simplify) seen as a contest between pro-American and pro-Communist tendencies. A small and honourable tendency argued for a 'third way' or 'third force' between both tendencies: it lost all influence when the Two Camps finally took up their adversary stance.

As a general rule, the pro-American, or Atlanticist tendency won, and the pro-Communist tendency was expelled or reduced to a grumbling opposition. But victorious Atlanticism placed Social-Democracy in an odd position. It entailed the submission of Social-Democratic and of Labour parties to the hegemony of the most vigorous capitalist power in the world military, diplomatic, and even in some economic, political and cultural affairs. This did not extinguish the humanitarian impulse in the programmes of those parties. So long as the economies continued to grow, it was possible, despite this overarching hegemony, to re-distribute some wealth within the native economy, and to assert some priorities in the fields of welfare, health or education. It was possible to keep electorates—and party activists—satisfied.

This is no longer possible. The reasons are self-evident. Some are directly economic: recession no longer affords space for humanitarian programmes, while it also stimulates direct competition between United States and EEC economies. Others are ideological: there has been a resurgence of the uninhibited reproductive drives of capital, from its United States strongholds, taking directly imperialist forms in its pursuit of oil, uranium, scarce resources and markets in the Second and Third Worlds, and propping up client military tyrannies. These reasons alone might have brought Atlanticism to the point of crisis. But the crisis, today, is above all political and military.

It no longer makes any sense for American hegemony to be extended over Western Europe through the institutions of NATO when, in the intervening thirty-five years since the Cold War set in, the balance of real forces has tipped back perceptibly towards this side of the Atlantic. It makes no sense at all for decisions as to the siting of missiles—and as to the ownership and operation of American missiles on European soil—to be taken in the Pentagon, when these decisions affect the very survival of Europe.

I have crossed the Atlantic a good many times in the past 15 years; and I can testify that, while the flight-time is getting less, the Atlantic ocean is getting wider. The United States has many virtues, and, among these, it is a more open, less secretive, less stuffy society than our own. But its political culture is now at an immense distance from that of Western Europe. It is, for example, the only major advanced society which has never had a political Labour movement, or Social-Democratic party, participating directly in national government. Its electorate is apathetic, and each successive President, in the past four elections, has been returned by a steadily declining proportion of the eligible electorate. President Reagan came to power with the support of little more than one-quarter of the possible total.

American political life in the past two decades has been vulgarised (I am tempted to say brutalised) and domesticated: that is, increasingly subordinated to the demands of domestic log-rolling. The average American citizen learns nothing of European affairs in his local newspaper or on his local TV channels. The present United States administration is, in its preoccupation with domestic issues and with domestic public image, effectively isolationist in its mentality; but it is an isolationism armed with nukes. Military muscle, nuclear weapons, are seen as a substitute for, not a supplement to, diplomacy.

How is a European Atlanticist today to bring any influence to bear upon such an administration? No Senators or Congressmen for Europe sit in Washington. Nor can they deliver any votes to the President, and ask for little services in return. When President Reagan wanted to site the MX missile on its giant tracks in Nevada and Utah he was forced to back away because he was losing the support of hard-core Republican electors. The Senator for the state of Nevada was one of his own political inner-set. But Chancellor Schmidt and Mrs Thatcher (if she were ever to harbour an un-American thought) are not part of his set. West Germany or Britain may be in an uproar about cruise missiles, but they have no voices in the Presidential electoral college.

It is this tension which is pulling Western European political formations–and especially those of Social-Democracy–apart. Atlanticism has outlived the rationale of its moment of formation: neither the socialist nor the European liberal tradition can consort easily any more with an overarching American hegemony, whose priorities are, ever more nakedly, determined by the reproductive needs of American capital. Some European socialist parties have simply opted out. The Spanish Socialists are now campaigning to revoke the entry of Spain into NATO, and in Greece the victorious socialist party, PASOK, is committed to expel US nuclear bases. In other countries–West Germany, Britain –the battle has been joined *within* the parties. It is the issue of Atlanticism, and not the issues which the media favour–constitutional squabbles, the personality of Tony Benn–which has contributed most to the formation of the British Social Democratic Party and the continuing conflicts within the Parliamentary Labour Party. An inherited ideological formation, an Atlanticist dogma, has come under challenge; the challengers are not pro-Soviet although they are the inheritors of the grumblers and the third wayers who lost out at the Cold War's origins; they are looking for a new alternative, but they cannot yet spell its name.

What, then, is the Cold War, as we enter the 1980s, *about?* The answer to this question can give us no comfort at all. If we look at the military scene, then nothing is receding. On the contrary, the military establishments of both superpowers continue to grow each year. The Cold War, in this sense, has broken free from the occasions at its origin, and has acquired an independent inertial thrust of its own. What is the Cold War now about? It is about itself.

We face here, in the grimmest sense, the 'consequences of consequences'. The Cold War may be seen as a show which was put, by two rival entrepreneurs, upon the road in 1946 or 1947. The show has grown bigger and bigger; the entrepreneurs have lost control of it, as it has thrown up its own managers, administrators, producers and a huge supporting cast; these have a direct interest in its continuance, in its enlargement. Whatever happens, the show must go on.

The Cold War has become a habit, an addiction. But it is a habit supported by very powerful material interests in each bloc: the military-industrial and research establishments of both sides, the security services and intelligence operations, and the political servants of these interests. These interests command a large (and growing) allocation of the skills and resources of each society; they influence the direction of each society's economic and social development; and it is in the interest *of* these interests to increase that allocation and to influence this direction even more.

I don't mean to argue for an *identity* of process in the United States and the Soviet Union, nor for a perfect symmetry of forms. There are major divergencies, not only in political forms and controls, but also as between the steady expansionism of bureaucracy and the avarice of private capital. I mean to stress, rather, the *reciprocal* and inter-active character of the process. It is in the very nature of this Cold War show that there must be two adversaries: and each move by one must be matched by the other. This is the inner dynamic of the Cold War which determines that its military and security establishments are *self-reproducing*. Their missiles summon forward our missiles which summon forward their missiles in turn. NATO's hawks feed the hawks of the Warsaw bloc.

For the ideology of the Cold War is self-reproducing also. That is, the military and the security services and their political servants *need* the Cold War. They have a direct interest in its continuance.

This is not only because their own establishments and their own careers depend upon this. It is not only because ruling groups can only justify their own privileges and their allocation of huge resources to 'defence' in the name of Cold War emergencies. And it is not only because the superpowers both need repeated Cold War alarms to keep their client states, in NATO or the Warsaw Pact, in line. All these explanations have force. But, at an even deeper level, there is a further explanation—which I will describe by the ugly word 'psycho-ideological'—which must occasion the grimmest pessimism.

The threat of an enemy—even recourse to war—has always afforded to uneasy rulers a means of internal ideological regulation and social discipline. This was a familiar notion to Shakespeare. The dying Henry IVth, knowing that the succession was beset with enemies, advised his son—

> Therefore, my Harry,
> Be it thy course to busy giddy minds
> With foreign quarrels. . .

This advice led Henry Vth to Agincourt.

The fear or threat of the Other is grounded upon a profound and universal human need. It is intrinsic to human bonding. We cannot define whom 'we' are without also defining 'them'—those who are not 'us'. 'They' need not be perceived as threatening: they may be seen only as different from 'us'—from our family, our community, our nation: 'they' are others who do not 'belong'. But if 'they' are seen as threatening to us, then our own internal bonding will be all the stronger.

This bonding-by-exclusion is intrinsic to human socialisation. 'Love and Hate', William Blake wrote, 'are necessary to Human existence.' This will not go away because we do not think it nice. It is present in every strong human association: the family, the church or political party, in class formation and class consciousness. Moreover, this bonding-by-exclusion establishes not only the identity of a group, but some part of the self-identity of the individuals within it. We belong to a family, we are citizens of Worcester, we are middle class or working class, we are members of a party, we are British: and some of this is internalised, it is our own identity.

Throughout history, as bonding has gone on and as identities have changed, the Other has been necessary to this process. Rome required barbarians, Christendom required pagans, Protestant and Catholic Europe required each other. The nation state bonded itself against other nations. Patriotism is love of one's own country; but it is also hatred or fear or suspicion of others.

This is not, in itself, a pessimistic finding, since we have developed every strong regulatory or counter-vailing influences to inhibit the aggressive constituent in bonding. We have 'civilised' ourselves, sometimes with success. In the early 19th century, a stranger or 'outcomling' walking through Lancashire might be hooted or pelted with stones. Or if a lad were to court a girl in the next village, in the West Riding, he might expect to be beaten up or driven out by the local youths. We do better today. We sublimate these aggressions in pop concerts or in football crowds. New racial conflicts in our society are alarming, but we do not despair of overcoming these ugly tensions also. We can even co-exist, except in disputed fishing-grounds or in academic philosophy, with the French.

Yet let us not take comfort too easily. War has been a constant recourse throughout history. It is an event as common in the human record as are nettles in the hedgerows. Despite all our 'civilisation' this century has seen already the two bloodiest wars in history, both engendered in the continent which prides itself most upon its civilised forms.

Let us return to today's Cold War. I have argued that the condition of the Cold War has broken free from the 'causes' at its origin: and that ruling interests on both sides have become ideologically addicted, they need its continuance. The Western hemisphere has been divided into two parts, each of which sees itself as threatened by the Other; yet at the same time this continuing threat has become necessary to provide internal bonding and social discipline within each part.

Moreover, this threat of the Other has been internalised within both Soviet and American culture, so that the very self-identity of many American and Soviet citizens is bound up with the ideological premises of the Cold War.

There are historical reasons for this, which have less to do with the actualities of communist or capitalist societies than we may suppose. Americans, for a century or so, have had a growing problem of national identity. America has a population, dispersed across half a continent, gathered in from the four corners of the globe. Layer upon layer of immigrants have come in, and new layers are being laid down today: Vietnamese and Thailanders, Cubans and undocumented Hispanic workers. Internal bonding tends to fall, not upon horizontal nationwide lines–the bonding of social class remains weak–but in vertical, fissiparous ways: local, regional, or ethnic bonding–the blacks, the Hispanics, the Poles, the Irish, the Jewish lobby. The resounding, media-propagated myth of United States society is that of an open market society, an upwardly-mobile free-for-all: its objective not any communal goal but equality of ego-fulfilment for everyone.

But where, in all these centrifugal and individualistic forces, is any national bonding and sense of American self-identity to be found? American poets and novelists have suggested better answers–America (they have suggested) might be the most internationalist nation in the world–but the answer which has satisfied America's present rulers is, precisely, in the Cold War. The United States is the leader of 'the Free World', and the Commies are the Other. They need this Other to establish their own identity, not as blacks or Poles or Irish, but as free Americans. Only this pre-existent need, for bonding-by-exclusion, can explain the ease by which one populist rascal after another has been able to float to power–and even to the White House–on nothing but a flood of sensational Cold War propaganda. And anti-Communism can be turned to other internal uses as well. It can serve to knock trade unions on the head, or to keep dissident radical voices or peace movements ('soft on Communism') on the margins of political life.

But what about the Soviet Union? Is there a similar need to bond against the Other within Soviet culture? I can speak with less confidence here. But there are indications that this is so.

The Soviet Union is not 'Russia' but a ramshackle empire inherited from Tsarist times. It also has its own fissiparous tendencies, from Mongolia to the Baltic states. It has no need to invent an Other, in some fit of paranoia. It has been struck within active memory, by another, to the gates of Moscow, with a loss of some 20 million dead. One would suppose that Soviet rulers, while having good reason for a defensive mentality, would need the Cold War like a hole in the head. They would want it to go away. And, maybe, some of them do.

Yet the Cold War, as ideology, has a bonding function in the Soviet Union also. This huge collocation of peoples feels itself to be surrounded–it is surrounded–from Mongolia to the Arctic ice-cap to its Western frontiers. The bonding, the self-identity, of Soviet citizens comes from the notion that they are the heartland of the world's first socialist revolution, threatened by the Other–Western imperialism, in alliance with 1,000 million Chinese. The positive part of this rhetoric–the Marxist-Leninist, revolutionary bit–may now have worn exceedingly thin; but the negative part remains compelling. The one function of the Soviet rulers which commands consensual assent throughout the population is their self-proclaimed role as defenders of the Fatherland and defenders of peace.

There is nothing sinister about that. But the bonding function of Cold War ideology in the Soviet Union is directly disciplinary. The threat of the Other legitimates every measure of policing or intellectual control. In Stalin's time this took the form of indiscriminate terror against 'counter-revolutionaries'. The measures of terror or of discipline have now been greatly modified. This is important and this is hopeful. But the function of this disciplinary ideology remains the same.

What it does is to transform every social or intellectual conflict within the Soviet Union into a problem affecting the security of the state. Every critic of Soviet reality, every 'dissident', is defined as an ally of the Other: as alien, unpatriotic, and perhaps as an agent of the West. Every impulse towards democracy or autonomy in Eastern Europe–the Prague Spring of 1968, the Polish renewal–is defined as a security threat to the Soviet frontiers and to the defensive unity of the Warsaw powers.

Like the populist American denunciation of 'Commies', the Soviet denunciation of 'Western' penetration can be turned to every purpose imaginable in the attempt to impose internal discipline:—but with the important difference that in the Soviet Union the attacks of the media and of political leaders are supplemented by more powerful and more intrusive security forces. Even juvenile delinquency, or the new wave of consumerism in the Soviet white-collar and professional groups can be denounced as Western attempts to 'subvert' Soviet society. And General Semyon Tsvigun, first deputy chairman of the KGB, writing recently in *Kommunist*, has instanced the 'negative influence' of Western styles and pop music upon Soviet young people as examples of the 'subversive' activities of the external 'class enemy'.

This is the double-bind which the Soviet people cannot break through. It is weary, but it works. And it works because the Cold Warriors of the West are eager to be in the same card-game, and to lead into the strong suits of their partners, the Cold Warriors of the East. The Western Warriors, by championing the cause of 'human rights', in the same moment define the dissidents of the East as allies of the West and as security risks. It is a hypocritical championship on several counts, but we will leave this aside. It is utterly counter-productive, and perhaps it is intended to be so. It does no-one, except the Cold Warriors of the other side, any good.

The boycott of the Moscow Olympics is a case in point. Initially this may have been welcomed by some dissident intellectuals in Eastern Europe and among some Soviet Jews. It was to do them no good. A Russian friend tells me that, as an operation promoting liberty, it was a disaster. The boycott bonded the Soviet people against the Other. In a state of siege and isolation for half-a-century, the Olympics offered to open international doors and to give them, for the first time, the role of host on the world stage. They were aggrieved, by the boycott, not as Communists, but in their latent patriotism. They had allocated resources to the Olympics, they had rehearsed their dancers and their choirs. They were curious to meet the world's athletes and visitors. Critics of the Olympics were felt to be disloyal, not only by the security services, but also by their workmates and neighbours. The boycott hence made possible the greatest crack-down upon all centres of critical opinion in the Soviet Union in a decade. It was a gift, from the CIA to the KGB. Lord Killanan and the British Olympic team, who ignored President Carter and Mrs Thatcher, did the right thing, not only in support of the Olympic tradition but also in support of the cause of peace. But 'dissent' in the Soviet Union has not yet recovered from the Western Cold Warriors' kind attentions.

It can be seen now, also, why the most conservative elements in the Soviet leadership—the direct inheritors of Stalin—*need* the Cold War. This is not only because some part of this leadership has arisen from, or spent some years in the service of, the bureaucratic-military-security complex itself. And it is not only because the very heavy allocations to defence, running to perhaps 15 per cent of the gross national product, must be justified in the eyes of the deprived public. It is also because these leaders are beset on every side by difficulties, by pressures to modernise, to reform or to democratise. Yet these pressures threaten their own position and privileges—once commenced, they might pass beyond control. The Polish renewal will have been watched, in the Soviet Union and in other Eastern European states, as an awful example of such a process—a process bringing instability and, with this, a threat to the security of the Communist world.

Hence Cold War ideology—the threat of the Other—is the strongest card left in the hand of the Soviet rulers. It is necessary for bonding. And the card is not a fake. For the Other—that is, the Cold Warriors of the West—is continually playing the same card back, whether in missiles or in arms agreements with China or in the suit of human rights.

We could not have led up to a more pessimistic conclusion. I have argued that the Cold War is now about itself. It is an ongoing, self-reproducing condition, to which both adversaries are addicted. The military establishments of the adversaries are in a reciprocal relationship of mutual nurture: each fosters the growth of the other. Both adversaries need to maintain a hostile ideological posture, as a means of internal bonding or discipline. This would be dangerous at any time; but with today's nuclear weaponry it is an immensely dangerous condition. For it contains a built-in logic which must always tend to the worse: the military establishments will grow, the adversary postures become more implacable and more irrational.

That logic, if uncorrected, must prove terminal, and in the next two or three decades. I will not speculate on what accident or which contingency will bring us to that terminus. I am pointing out the logic and thrust of things, the current which is sweeping us towards Niagara Falls. As we go over those Falls we may comfort ourselves that it was really no-one's fault: that human culture has always contained within itself a malfunction, a principle of bonding-by-exclusion which must (with our present technologies of death) lead to auto-destruct. We might have guessed as much by looking at the nettles in history's hedges.

All this perhaps will happen. I think it at least probable that it will. We cannot expect to have the good fortune of having our planet invaded, in the 1990s, by some monsters from outer space, who would at last bond all humanity against an outer Other. And short of some science-fiction rescue operation like that, all proposals look like wish-fulfilment.

Yet I would ask you to cast your minds back to the considerations in the earlier part of this lecture. I have offered you a contradiction. I argued, at first, that a whole era of Cold War might be drawing to an end. Today's military confrontation is protracted long after the historical occasion for it has come to an end. And my argument here is close to a recent editorial comment in the London *Times* (2 October 1981):

> The huge accumulations of weaponry which the two brandish at each other are wholly out of proportion to any genuine conflict of interests. There is no serious competition for essential resources, or for territory that is truly vital to the security of either, and the ideological fires have dwindled on both sides. In strictly objective terms a reasonable degree of accommodation should be easily attainable.

But I argued, subsequently, that the Cold War, as adversary military establishments and adversary ideological posture, was an on-going, self-reproducing road-show, which had become necessary to ruling groups on both sides. Can we find, within that contradiction, any resolution short of war?

Perhaps we can. But the resolution will not be easy. A general revolt of reason and conscience against the instruments which immediately threaten us—a lived perception, informing multitudes, of the human ecological imperative: this is a necessary part of the answer. Such a revolt, such a shift in perception, is already growing across Europe. But this cannot be the whole answer. For if the Cold War has acquired a self-generating dynamic, then, as soon as public concern is quietened by a few measures of arms control, new dangers and new weapons will appear. We must do more than protest if we are to survive. We must go behind the missiles to the Cold War itself. We must begin to put Europe back into one piece.

And how could that be done? Very certainly it can not be done by the victory of one side over the other. That would mean war. We must retrace our steps to that moment, in 1944, before glaciation set in, and look once again for a third way.

If I had said this two years ago I would have despaired of holding your attention. But something remarkable is stirring in this continent today; movements which commenced in fear and which are now taking on the shape of hope; movements which cannot yet, with clarity, name their own demands. For the first time since the wartime Resistance there is a spirit abroad in Europe which carries a trans-continental aspiration. The Other which menaces us is being redefined—not as other nations, nor even as the other bloc, but as the forces leading both blocs to auto-destruction—not 'Russia' nor 'America' but their military, ideological and security establishments and their ritual oppositions.

And at the same time, as this Other is excluded, so a new kind of internal bonding is taking place. This takes the form of a growing commitment, by many thousands, to the imperative of survival and against the ideological or security imperatives of either bloc or their nation-states. In the words of the Appeal for European Nuclear Disarmament of April 1980:

We must commence to act as if a united, neutral and pacific Europe already exists. We must learn to be loyal, not to 'East' or 'West', but to each other.

This is a large and improbable expectation. It has often been proclaimed in the past, and it has been as often disappointed. Yet what is improbable has already, in the past year, begun to happen. The military structures are under challenge. But something is happening of far greater significance. The ideological structures are under challenge also, and from *both* sides.

I said, at the beginning, that the Cold War had placed the political culture of Europe in a permanent double-bind: the cause of 'peace' and the cause of 'freedom' fell apart. What is now happening is that these two causes are returning to one cause—peace *and* freedom—and as this happens, so, by a hundred different channels, the transcontinental discourse of political culture can be resumed.

The peace movements which have developed with such astonishing rapidity in Northern, Western and Southern Europe—and which are now finding an echo in the East—are one part of this cause. They have arisen in response not only to a military and strategic situation but to a political situation also. What has aroused Europeans most is the spectacle of two superpowers, arguing above their heads about the deployment of weapons whose target would be the 'theatre' of Europe. These movements speak with new accents. They are, in most cases, neither pro-Soviet nor manipulated by the Communist-influenced World Peace Council. Their objective is to clear nuclear weapons and bases out of the whole continent, East and West, and then to roll back conventional forces. Nor is it correct to describe them as 'neutralist' or 'pacifist'. They are looking for a third way. A third way is an active way: it is not 'neutral' between the other ways, it goes somewhere else.

The Western peace movements, in majority opinion, bring together traditions—socialist, trade unionist, liberal, Christian, ecological—which have always been committed to civil rights. They extend their support to the Polish renewal and to Solidarity, and to movements of libertarian dissent in the

Warsaw bloc. And from Eastern Europe also, voice after voice is now reaching us–hesitant, cautious, but with growing confidence–searching for the same alliance: peace *and* freedom.

These voices signal that the whole thirty-five-year-old era of the Cold War could be coming to an end: the Ice Age could give way to turbulent torrents running from East to West and from West to East. And within the demands of the peace movements and also in movements of lower profile but of equal potential in Eastern Europe there is maturing a further–and a convergent–demand: to shake off the hegemony of the superpowers and to reclaim autonomy.

This demand was glimpsed by Dr Albert Schweitzer in a notable broadcast appeal from Oslo in April, 1958:

> Today America with her batteries of nuclear rockets in Europe is present with mighty military power in Europe. Europe has become an in-between land between America and Russia, as if America by some displacement of a continent had come closer to her. But if atomic rockets were no longer in question, this unnatural state of affairs would come to an end. America would again become wholly America; Europe wholly Europe; the Atlantic again wholly the Atlantic Ocean–a sea providing distance in time and space.
>
> In this way could come the beginning of the end of America's military presence in Europe, a presence arising from the two world wars. The great sacrifices that America made for Europe during the Second World War, and in the years following it, will not be forgotten; the great and varied help that Europe received from her, and the thanks owing for this, will not be forgotten. But the unnatural situation created by the two world wars that led to a dominating military presence in Europe cannot continue indefinitely. It must gradually cease to exist, both for the sake of Europe and for the sake of America.
>
> Now there will be shocked voices from all sides. What will become of poor Europe if American atomic weapons no longer defend it from within and from without? What will happen if Europe is delivered to the Soviet? Must it then not be prepared to languish in a communist babylonian form of imprisonment for long years?
>
> Here it should be said that perhaps the Soviet Union is not quite so malicious as to think only of throwing itself on Europe at the first opportunity in order to devour it, and perhaps not quite so unintelligent as to fail to consider whether there would be any

advantage in upsetting her stomach with this indigestible meal.

What Europe and the Europeans have to agree is that they belong together for better or for worse. This is a new historical fact that can no longer be by-passed politically.

Albert Schweitzer argued this, twenty-three years ago, from the perspective of a West European. In the long interval that has now passed it is possible to make this same argument from an Eastern European perspective also. We no longer speculate upon the old ambition of John Foster Dulles–the 'West' *liberating* the 'East'. Eastern Europe has commenced its own self-liberation. In cautious ways, Roumania, Hungary and East Germany have established small areas of autonomy, of foreign policy, economy or culture, while the Polish renewal signals a social transition so swift and far-reaching that speculation upon its outcome is futile. In Czechoslovakia, where social renewal was ruthlessly reversed in 1968, the hegemony of Soviet military power remains decisive. But here also courageous voices of dissent are beginning to consider a strategy in which the cause of freedom and the cause of peace can draw strength from each other as allies.

On November 16th, 1981, there was issued in Prague a statement by three spokespersons of Charter 77, the courageous organisation defending Czechoslovak human rights: Václav Malý, Dr Bedrich Placák, and Dr Jiri Hájek. This stresses the mutual interdependence of the causes of peace and of liberty. The Helsinki accord on human rights is an 'integral and equal component' of the cause of peace, since without respect for these rights 'it is impossible to speak of an attitude to peace worthy of the name'. Yet (the statement continues) 'it is difficult to regard as genuine champions of these rights and freedoms those who are stepping up the arms race and bringing closer the danger of war.' 'Our continent faces the threat of being turned into a nuclear battlefield, into the burial-ground of its nations and its civilisation which gave birth to the very concept of human rights.' And it concludes by expressing the solidarity of Charter 77 with all those in the peace movement who are also upholding the rights endorsed by the Helsinki accord:

It is our wish that they should continue their struggle for peace in its indivisibility, which not only applies to different geographic regions but also covers the various dimensions of human life. We do not have the opportunities which they have to express as loudly our common conviction that peace and freedom are indivisible.

The question before Europeans today is not how many NATO forward-based systems might equal how many Soviet SS-20s. Beneath these equations there is a larger question: in what circumstances might *both* superpowers loosen the military grip which settled upon Europe in 1945 and which has been protracted long beyond its historical occasion? And how might such a retreat of hegemonies and loosening of blocs take place without endangering peace? Such an outcome would be profoundly in the interest, not only of the people of Europe, but of the peoples of the Soviet Union and the United States also—in relaxing tension and in relieving them of some of the burdens and dangers of their opposed military establishments. But what—unless it were to be our old enemy 'deterrence'—could monitor such a transition so that neither one nor the other party turned it to advantage?

We are not, it should be said, describing some novel stage in the process known as 'detente'. For in the early 1970s 'detente' signified the cautious tuning-down of hostilities between states or blocs, but within the Cold War *status quo*. Detente (or 'peaceful co-existence') was licensed by the superpowers: it did not arise from the client states, still less from popular movements. The framework of East-West settlement was held rigid by 'deterrence': in the high noon of Kissinger's diplomacy detente was a horse-trade between the leaders of the blocs, in which any unseemly movement out of the framework was to be discouraged as 'de-stabilising'. Czechs or Italians were required to remain quiet in their client places, lest any rash movement should disturb the tetchy equilibrium of the superpowers.

But what we can glimpse now is something different: a detente of peoples rather than states—a movement of peoples which sometimes dislodges states from their blocs and brings them into a new diplomacy of conciliation, which sometimes runs beneath state structures, and which sometimes defies the ideological and security structures of particular states. This will be a more fluid, unregulated, unpredictable movement. It may entail risk.

The risk must be taken. For the Cold War can be brought to an end in only two ways: by the destruction of European civilisation, or by the reunification of European political culture. The first will take place if the ruling groups in the rival superpowers, sensing that the ground is shifting beneath them and that their client states are becoming detached, succeed in compensating for their waning political and economic authority by more and more frenzied measures of militarisation. This is, exactly, what is happening now. The outcome will be terminal.

But we can now see a small opening towards the other alternative. And if we thought this alternative to be possible, then we should–every one of us–re-order all our priorities. We would invest nothing more in missiles, everything in all the skills of communication and exchange.

When I first offered a synopsis of this lecture to the BBC, I promised 'some practical proposals and even a programme, as to how this could be done'. But I realise now that, even if time permitted, such a programme would be over-ambitious. This cannot be written by any one citizen, in Worcester. It must be written by many hands–in Warsaw and in Athens, in Berlin and in Prague. All I can do now is indicate, briefly, programmes which are already in the making.

One such programme is that of limited nuclear-free zones. I have the honour to speak now in the Guildhall of the nuclear-free city of Worcester. I need not say here, Mr Mayor, that this is not just a gesture of self-preservation. It is a signal also, of international conciliation, and a signal which we hope will be reciprocated. Such signals are now arising across our continent. A Nordic nuclear-free zone is now under active consideration. And in the South-East of Europe, the incoming Greek government is pledged to initiate discussions with Bulgaria and Romania (in the Warsaw Pact) and with non-aligned Yugoslavia, for a further nuclear-free zone.

Such zones have political significance. Both states and local authorities can enlarge the notion to take in exchanges between citizens, for direct uncensored discourse. In Central Europe a zone of this kind might go further to take in measures of conventional disarmament also, and the withdrawal of both Soviet and NATO forces from both Germanys. This proposal is now being actively canvassed in East Germany as well as West–the East German civil rights supporter, Dr Robert Havemann has raised the question directly in an open letter to Mr Brezhnev–and is now being discussed, in unofficial circles, in Poland and Czechoslovakia as well.

The objectives of such larger zones are clear: to make a space of lessened tension between the two blocs: to destroy the menacing symbolic affront of nuclear weapons: to bring nations both East and West within reciprocal agreements: and to loosen the bonds of the bloc system, allowing more autonomy, more initiative to the smaller states.

But at the same time there must be other initiatives, through a hundred different channels, by which citizens enlarge this discourse. It is absurd to expect the weapons systems of both sides to de-weaponise themselves, the security systems of both sides to fall into each other's arms. It is, precisely, at the top of the Cold War systems that deadlock, or worse, takes place. If we are to destructure the Cold War, then we must destabilise these systems from below.

I am talking of a new kind of politics which cannot (with however much goodwill) be conducted by politicians. It must be a politics of peace, informed by a new internationalist code of honour, conducted by citizens. And it is now being so conducted by the international medical profession, by churches, by writers and by many others.

Music can be a 'politics' of this kind. I will take an example from this city. We had the honour here, at the last Three Choirs Festival, to hear the first British performance of Sallinen's *Dies Irae.* This work is a setting of a poem about the threat to our planet from nuclear weapons by the Finnish poet, Arvo Turtianen, commissioned by the Ensemble of the Hungarian People's Army–I don't much like armies but I can't object to a military Ensemble which commissions a work on peace–first performed in Budapest, and then performed in our own city.

If this is a small, but beautiful, sound of reconciliation, then other sounds are large and loud. For across our continent the world of popular music is now making its own sounds of peace and freedom. There is, today, some generational cultural mutation taking place among the young people of Europe. The demonstrations for peace–Bonn, London, Madrid, Rome, Amsterdam–have been thronged with the young. The young are *bored* with the Cold War. There is a shift at a level below politics–expressed in style, in sound, in symbol, in dress–which could be more significant than any negotiations taking place in Geneva. The PA systems of these popular music bands are already capable of making transcontinental sounds. The bands may not be expert arms negotiators; but they might blast the youth of Europe into each others' arms.

It has been proposed that there might be a festival–it might be called 'Theatre of Peace'–somewhere in Central Europe in the summer of 1983. Young people (although their elders would not be excluded) would be called to assemble from every part of the continent, bringing with them their music, their living theatre, their art, their posters, their symbols and gifts. There would be rallies, workshops, and informal discussions. Every effort would be made to invite youth from 'the other side', not in pre-selected official parties but as individual visitors and strays. For 1982 the project may be too ambitious: but as a 'primer' for this plans are now afoot for a popular music festival of peace at a site close to Vienna early in August 1982. Already the first responses to the plan are such that the problem is one of keeping the numbers within the limits requested by hospitable Austrian authorities.

I return, in my conclusion, to the most sensitive, and the most significant, issue of all. How do we put the causes of freedom and of peace back together?

This cannot be done by provocative interventions in the affairs of other nations. And it certainly cannot be done by the old strategy of Cold War 'linkage'. If we look forward to democratic renewal on the other side of our common world, then this strategy is plainly counter-productive. No-one will ever obtain civil or trade union rights in the East because the West is pressing missiles against their borders. On the contrary, this only enhances the security operations and the security-minded ideology of their rulers. The peoples of the East, as of the West, will obtain their own rights and liberties for themselves and in their own way—as the Portuguese, Spanish, Greek and Polish people have shown us. What is needed, from and for all of us, is a space free of Cold War crisis in which we can move.

There might, however, be a very different kind of citizen's linkage in which, as part of the people's detente, the movement for peace in the West and for freedom in the East recognised each other as natural allies. For this to be possible, we in the West must move first. As the military pressure upon the East begins to relax, so the old double-bind would begin to lose its force. And the Western peace movement (which can scarcely be cast convincingly by Soviet ideologists as an 'agent of Western imperialism') should press steadily upon the state structures of the East demands for greater openness of exchange, both of persons and of ideas.

A transcontinental discourse must begin to flow, in both directions, with the peace movement—a movement of unofficial persons with a code of conduct which disallows the pursuit of political advantage for either 'side'—as the conduit. We cannot be content to criticise nuclear missiles. We have to be, in every moment, critics also of the adversary posture of the powers. For we are threatened, not only by weapons, but by the ideological and security structures which divide our continent and which turn us into adversaries. So that the concession which the peace movement asks of the Soviet state is—not so much these SS-20s and those Backfire bombers—but its assistance in commencing to tear these structures down. And in good time one might look forward to a further change, in the Soviet Union itself, as the long-outworn ideology and structures inherited from Stalin's time gave way before internal pressures for a Soviet renewal.

It is optimistic to suppose so. Yet this is the only way in which the Cold War could be brought to an end. I have also conceded that an end of glaciation—with new and turbulent torrents across the East-West divide—will entail new risks. We have observed this for a year as the Polish crisis has unfolded. To those who have been habituated to Cold War stasis this looks like dangerous 'instability'.

Yet I will argue, against these critics, that in such an emergency the peace movement itself may prove to be the strongest force making for stability. Only a non-aligned peace movement could moderate this great social transition, enabling our political cultures to grow back together, and restraining both NATO and Warsaw power rulers from intervening to check the change or from seeking to gain advantage from the discomforture of the other side. The peace movement must say–and has already been saying–'Let Poland be Polish and let Greece be Greek!'

We may be living now, and in the next few years, in the very eye of crisis. The Cold War road-show, which each year enlarges, is now lurching towards its terminus. But in this moment changes have arisen in our continent, of scarcely more than one year's growth, which signify a challenge to the Cold War itself. These are not 'political' changes, in the usual sense. They cut through the flesh of politics down to the human bone.

Dr Nicholas Humphrey, in his remarkable Bronowski lecture, warned us of one possible outcome. I have been proposing another. What I have proposed is improbable. But, if it commenced, it might gather pace with astonishing rapidity. There would not be decades of detente, as the glaciers slowly melt. There would be very rapid and unpredictable changes; nations would become unglued from their alliances; there would be sharp conflicts within nations; there would be successive risks. We could roll up the map of the Cold War, and travel without maps for a while.

I do not mean that Russia would become a Western democracy, nor that the West would go Communist. Immense differences in social system would remain. Nations, unglued from their alliances, might–as Poland and Greece are now showing us–fall back more strongly into their own inherited national traditions. I mean only that the flow of political and intellectual discourse, and of human exchange, would resume across the whole continent. The blocs would discover that they had forgotten what their adversary posture was about.

Where Dr Humphrey and I are united is in our conviction that we do not live in ordinary times. To work to bring the Cold War to an end is not one among three dozen things which we must remember to do. It must be, for tens of thousands of us in Europe in this decade, the first thing we must do; and it must inform everything we do.

Our species has been favoured on this planet, although we have not always been good caretakers of our globe's resources. Our stay here, in the spaces of geological time, has been brief. No-one can tell us our business. But I think it is something more than to consume as much as we can and then blow the place up.

We have, if not a duty, then a need, deeply engraved within our culture, to pass the place on no worse than we found it. Those of us who do not expect an after-life may see in this our only immortality: to pass on the succession of life, the succession of culture. It may even be that we are happier when we are engaged in matters larger than our own wants and ourselves.

We did not choose to live in this time. But there is no way of getting out of it. And it has given to us as significant a cause as has ever been known, a moment of opportunity which might never be renewed. If these weapons and then those weapons are added to the huge sum on our continent—if Poland drifts into civil war and if this calls down Soviet military intervention—if the United States launches some military adventure in the Middle East—can we be certain that this moment will ever come back? I do not think so. If my analysis is right, then the inertial thrust of the Cold War, from its formidable military and ideological bases, will have passed the point of no return.

The opportunity is *now,* when there is already an enhanced consciousness of danger informing millions. We can match this crisis only by a summoning of resources to a height like that of the greatest religious or political movement's of Europe's past. I think, once again, of 1944 and of the crest of the Resistance. There must be that kind of spirit abroad in Europe once more. But this time it must arise, not in the wake of war and repression, but before these take place. Five minutes afterwards, and it will be too late.

Humankind must at last grow up. We must recognise that the Other is ourselves.

THE WAR OF THATCHER'S FACE

I am ready to stand up and be counted as one of those who is utterly disgusted with the Argentine regime and with its actions. Argentina has long been known as a place of refuge, not only for the odd Nazi war criminal, but also for odious fascist ideologies.

When I was in the United States last year a sensation was created by the publication of Jacob Timerman's *Prisoner Without a Name, Cell Without a Number.* It will be recalled that this independent-minded radical editor was one of those thousands who became lost, for several years, in the torture-cellars of the Argentinian security police, and that he was lucky to emerge alive. One of his offences is to have been a Jew, and he recalls interrogators dressed in Nazi style and a cellar with Hitler's portrait on the wall.

That is not a nice regime. It is not, in fact, the kind of regime I would sell arms to. Perhaps the Foreign Office has only just got around to reading Mr Timerman's book. Or, maybe, in the present state of the economy—and in view of our desperate need to earn money to buy Trident—we were left with no choice.

But this was not Mr Timerman's point. He was over-excited when he wrote his book, which is understandable in a man who has been cut off in the darkness and tortured on various parts, including his genitals, for a year or two. His point was that some Western publicists and even some New York Jewish intellectuals had suppressed the evidence of Argentinian anti-Semitism and tyranny because the abuse of human rights was in the wrong part of the world and was committed against the wrong victims. It did not fit

---

This article first appeared in *The Times*, 29 April 1982.

conveniently into the authorised Cold War script. For a certain kind of 'Committee for the Free World' lobby the repression of rights of Soviet Jews made much better copy. And who knows? Might not Mr Timerman have formed some indiscreet associations, perhaps with Communists, and have brought all this trouble on himself?

Argentina is, after all, only a country in the third division, and it is better not to look into the affairs of such countries too closely. 'Authoritarian' regimes (as Mrs Kirkpatrick, the US Ambassador to the United Nations, has patiently explained) are a very different matter from 'totalitarian' ones. *Their* regimes are totalitarian: but smelly regimes which are on *our* side in the Cold War are only authoritarian. President Allende's regime in Chile did not get sent large economic credits or military aircraft and had, in the end, to be destabilised because it *might have become* a totalitarian regime, although (as it happens) it did not.

It is confusing, but with patience the point can be understood. And it has been absolutely clear for some years to both the British and American authorities that the Argentine regime has been completely sound in that kind of way—not totalitarian at all. Indeed, quite a few Argentinian Communists, trade unionists and socialists have shared Mr Timerman's experience of cellars, and not many have come out.

Mr Timerman became excessively excited when he heard this kind of argument. He even had the vulgarity to exclaim that he would be willing, for one time more, to be tortured on his genitals if it was done on full television before the American public, and if this might bring Americans to a better understanding of the nature of a regime which has received so much succour from their own government. One can see why the Argentinians had to take such an excitable fellow in hand. He had not understood Mrs Kirkpatrick's point at all.

Nor had he understood the importance of the Argentine state as a customer. As one scans an inventory of the Argentine air and sea forces it has a reassuring kind of feel. It is a compendium of the arsenal of the Free World. There is a British carrier and an American cruiser: two British destroyers and six from the USA: the corvettes come from France and the submarines equally from Germany and the United States. There are some British Canberras: some Boeing 707s marshalled against the British Navy's own Boeing Chinook helicopters (whoever loses, Boeing will win this war); some French Mirages and Etendards, and various Daggers and reach-me-downs from Israel (whose Foreign Office has mislaid Mr Timerman's book). The Skyhawks are from the United States, but the bombs they carry may, for all I know, have been sent with the compliments of our own Ministry of Defence. A little way behind, not to be unveiled this year, are Argentine nuclear weapons, helped on their way by West German expertise.

We have run up against something which it is usual to describe today as 'a wrinkle' but for which the Greeks had a better name. What will be descending shortly on our task-force in those wintry seas is a squadron of furies under the direct command of Admiral Nemesis. As the captain of an Israeli-built gunboat equipped with British radar and American weaponry remarked to a British correspondent: 'It will be interesting to fight them with their own weapons.'

Modesty prevents me from saying that some of us have been warning of the impending offensive of Nemesis for some time. The advanced world cannot go on pumping weaponry into the Third World and expect that world to stay the same. We cannot be certain that all these arms will be used only to kill their own people or to keep in order their own poor. It is not to be supposed that every gun can carry a guarantee that it will only go off against Her Majesty's certified enemies; or that all our customers will always engage in comfortable wars, like that between Iran and Iraq—wars which advance no interest save that of the armourers' trade. There are going to be many other wrinkles. The Falklands crisis is a sample of what we can expect to become commonplace.

All that is clear enough. As to the rest of the Falklands crisis I know even less than other loyal Britons because in its first ten days my wife and I were off in a part of Yugoslavia whose benefits included an absence of the British media. To return to England on Day 10 of the crisis was like passing through a time-warp into an earlier imperial age.

On every screen and in every editorial one encountered the aged Ulysses of Tennyson's imagination, preparing to set off on his final voyage:

> Tho' much is taken, much abides; and tho'
> We are not now that strength which in old days
> Moved earth and heaven; that which we are, we are;
> One equal temper of heroic hearts,
> Made weak by time and fate, but strong in will
> To strive, to seek, to find, and not to yield.

We found ourselves of a sudden back in the days of Dunkirk, replayed this time as a nostalgic period piece, with parliamentarians 'speaking for Britain', with chat-show chairmen conducting consensual exercises, with peers and politicians standing up to be counted and pointing their paunches at the cameras, with schoolboys packing the portholes to sing 'Rule Britannia', and with the fleet leaving the cheering quays of Portsmouth and standing off into a westering sun:

> Push off, and sitting well in order smite
> The sounding furrows; for my purpose holds
> To sail beyond the sunset and the paths
> Of all the Western stars until I die...

And what was this about? It was about something other than the Falkland Islands. It was something more—a moment of imperial atavism, drenched with the nostalgias of those now in their late middle-age: the officer class of my own generation. There is talk once more of landings on beaches, going it alone, and (sotto voce) keeping up the morale of the men. It was as if the need for a pageant of this kind had long been working itself up to the surface of the collective unconscious and the Falklands crisis gave it the pretext to come out.

Let us be clear, at least, as to what the Falklands crisis is not about. It is not about the interests of the Falklands islanders. Those who were able to get away upon ten minutes notice have already flown for their lives. They have been hustled out of the back exits to airports lest they should blurt out the self-evident truth—that a shooting war on their islands would destroy their homes, their livelihood, their neighbours' lives.

Even if the British are about to launch a heroic assault and reconquer the main islands, few of the islanders will wish to stay. The task force is not going to stop over there for ever, in those furious winter waters. NATO has other plans for it. Argentina will await the next moment of absent-mindedness in Whitehall and descend with the ferocity of injured national honour.

Falklanders who wish to remain inviolate and British citizens (which it was decided in Westminster not long ago they are not) are on a hiding to nowhere. They are too few. They are too far away. This is regrettable. But even paramountcy must have lines of supply.

The Falklands war is not about the islanders. It is about 'face'. It is about domestic politics. It is about what happens when you twist a lion's tail. The Argentine junta have been facing severe political unrest and want to whoop up support with a patriotic hullabaloo. The United States wants to appear before world opinion in the novel role of a peace-maker, while at the same time throwing one arm around its most subservient military client in Europe and the other around a sound authoritarian ally in Latin America. After all, the overthrow of the present junta in consequence of a national humiliation could open up a space for something 'worse'—perhaps even an elected government soft, like Allende, on 'totalitarianism'.

And Mrs Thatcher? She is watching, not the interests of the islanders, but her own back-benchers and the Gallup Polls. Her administration has lost a by-election in Glasgow and it needs to sink the Argentine navy in revenge.

Mrs Thatcher has boxed herself into a corner and there is no way out without blood. She will not wish to go down in history in the same verses as the noble Duke of York. She must bring her ten thousand men down the hill with a little more smoke and glory. Westminster has put this piece of theatre on, and now it must have—after a dull second act in which it was upstaged by General Haig—some colourful climax with piled bodies on the stage, some bugles, and the hauling up and down of flags. South Georgia is satisfactory, but it will not be enough. For a true imperial catharsis there will have to be more dead than that.

There is also the cost of the thing. It cannot be expected that the British people will go on willingly for ever, paying for the follies of their rulers. There has already been grumbling about the small matter of Chevaline and more about Trident. If the taxpayer is to stump up another one thousand millions for this technicolour production, then there will have to be a lot of Argentinian blood on the invoice.

The response to the Falklands crisis has been one of imperial atavism although the issue itself has not been one of imperial rule. The Falklands have not been an exploited colony: they have been forgotten and ignored. Mr Nott has been too busy selling off 'Invincible' and campaigning against CND to give their protection a thought; and it is he, and not Lord Carrington, who should have had the sense of honour to go. Those Soviet publicists who have been ranting about colonialism in order to ingratiate themselves with a fascist supplier of grain and beef are as contemptible as are the purveyors of the consensual cant on this side.

There is, to be sure, the question of off-shore oil, and the shadowy claims to the resources of Antarctica beyond. If this is what the affair is about (but I think that it is not) then it certainly is both imperialist and absurd. That claim, to resources in another hemisphere, will not be taken up as a just *casus belli* by anyone else in the world.

The Falkland Islands were taken by an act of aggression. The islanders were not 'liberated' from anyone's imperial rule. On this there could have been a force of world opinion. The aggression was censured by the United Nations. Whatever may have been the rights and wrongs of Argentina's claim, the manner of its assertion was deplored.

The British, if they had had the interests of the islanders at heart, would have built upon that building-block. Sanctions and diplomatic pressures might have afforded protection to the islanders—some intermediating United Nations trusteeship which could have stood between them and the junta.

It is not only that this has not been tried. It is that Mrs Thatcher, in preferring to fall back upon American brokerage and her own military menace, has thrown away the goodwill which, two weeks ago, would have made the attempt feasible. With the hostilities on South Georgia, with each new escalation of menace, the more Britain drags herself back, in the world's eyes, into the stereotypes of her own imperial history, and the more support for the islanders' case falls away.

And this is the work of Nemesis once more. It is because we have ceased to take the United Nations seriously as a peace-enforcing agency, ever since Third World voices multiplied and the votes began to go against us, that we have turned away from the legitimate and obvious recourse. In scouting its injunctions we have made the world an even more dangerous place. The UN might have done something but it might not have done exactly what Mrs Thatcher wished. We have signalled that it need be obeyed (if at all) only by lesser breeds without the law.

Whatever happens now, the islanders must be the losers. And the expedition, after a glorious episode or two, will also fail. At its imperial best it can only save, for a year or two, half an imperial face. And it could—but God forbid!—end in something far worse than that. What if some of that Argentinian hardware lived up to the glossy brochures of our own arms salesmen? What if a (US) Skyhawk bomber or a (British) Sea Dart of (French) Exocet missile should find its mark on one of our warships, pitching in unfamiliar waters off Cape Disappointment and packed to the gunwales with sick troops? By what right has either junta sent these young lives to risk in those fierce seas?

The Falklands war has shown us at least this—how close to the surface of our even-tenored life the atavistic moods of violence lie. We shall pay for it for a long time, in rapes and racism in our cities, in international ill-will, and in the stirring up of ugly nationalist sediment which will cloud our political and cultural life. Full war in the Falklands will be a general licence to disorder, a revocation of the rule of law, signed by the Prime Minister and to be paid for from the National Exchequer. As a contest for national 'face', an eyeball-to-eyeball confrontation in which neither party has yet swerved, it tells us all that we need to know about the behaviour of great persons of state, and the way in which, around some other issue, in some other year, we may drift into World War III.

As for the islanders, that is immeasurably sad. It ought to be possible for people to find, at the uttermost ends of the earth, some quiet sanctuary where they can pursue a modest livelihood in peace. And yet it is not so. There are no corners now that are utter enough. From the Falklands to Greenland, the globe has been tied up into one military knot.

Some of the Falklanders (I am told) are the descendants of crofters from the Western Isles, victims of the clearances of the last century. They deserved something better than another clearance. So do the descendants of their cousins who clung on in the Isles, and whose way-of-life is now threatened, not by Argentina, but by the NATO base to be built at Stornoway. The wishes of these islanders have been clearly expressed, by their own Island Council, but have been scouted by the Ministry of Defence. If I was to mount an expeditionary force it would be directed there. It would be unarmed.

ACKNOWLEDGEMENTS

My thanks are due to the newspapers and periodicals in which several of these essays first appeared: *The Times,* the *Guardian,* the *New Statesman, New Society, The Bulletin of the Atomic Scientists* and *New Left Review.*

'Deterrence and Addiction' is also published in *The Nuclear Arms Race: Control or Catastrophe,* edited by Frank Barnaby and Geoffrey Thomas, Frances Pinter (Publishers), London 1982, and my thanks are due to the editors and publishers. 'Notes on Exterminism' is appearing in a collection, *Exterminism and Cold War,* published by New Left Books, London 1982: this collection includes an international discussion of issues raised in my article, as well as many other issues, and a response from myself. 'Courtier at Toad Hall' also appears in *Debate on Disarmament,* edited by Michael Clarke and Marjorie Mowlam, Routledge & Kegan Paul, London 1982. 'Human Rights and Disarmament' has also been published, in pamphlet form, by the Spokesman Press, Nottingham.

'Beyond the Cold War' was first delivered as a lecture in Worcester City Guildhall on November 26th, 1981, on the invitation of a Worcester Citizens Group. It is an expanded version of the lecture which I would have delivered on the BBC if the original suggestion that I might give the 1981 Dimbleby Lecture had not been withdrawn. It was first published as a pamphlet by Merlin Press.

When 'The War of Thatcher's Face' appeared in *The Times* (April 29th, 1982) it was given a generous review in the House of Lords. Lord Beloff (C) said: 'I think this passes the bounds of decency in journalism (Cheers). It was not a thing which anyone, not even Mr E.P. Thompson, should have written, and having written it, it is not a thing which a great newspaper, read throughout the world, should have been willing to print (Cheers).' In view of this and similar judgments, I am grateful to *The Times* for exercising, at a time of national near-hysteria, its independent editorial decision to afford to me the space for a dissenting view. I can only add that–since this book is going to press with the issue still undecided–I hope most profoundly that my own more pessimistic predictions will prove (when this is published) to have been wrong.

My warm thanks also to all those who have helped on this book by advice and response–especially to those in the peace movement at home, in Europe and in the United States; to colleagues in the committee for European Nuclear Disarmament (END) and in CND; to Dorothy Thompson, Martin Eve and Dave Musson for their suggestions and criticisms; to Evelyn King for her help with typing and correspondence; and to Hedda Hems for typesetting 'Beyond the Cold War' as a gift to the movement.

I have also been encouraged, for more than two years, by a heavy correspondence and by many invitations to speak. I hope it will not be thought discourteous to say that this welcome response is now more than an individual can deal with? There are many local and national organisations which are working hard and effectively for peace. The ones which command my own particular support are END, 227 Seven Sisters Road, London N4, and CND, 11 Goodwin Street, London N4. Readers interested in the Vienna Peace Festival (August 6th–9th, 1982) should write for details to: Vienna Festival, Worthy Farm, Pilton, Nr Shepton Mallet, Somerset.

ABOUT THE AUTHOR

Edward Palmer Thompson was born in England, served in Africa and Italy during the war, and returned to England to graduate from Cambridge University. In 1957, he helped found the magazine *The New Reasoner;* he later served on the editorial board of *The New Left Review*. Since 1972 he has been working full-time at writing, with some spells of teaching in the United States (at Pittsburgh, Rutgers, and Brown universities) and in India.

In early 1980, E. P. Thompson drafted the Appeal for European Nuclear Disarmament, which, after much revision, was signed by many thousands of Europeans and became one of the platforms of the new peace movement. In Britain, he works actively with the Campaign for Nuclear Disarmament (CND) and with the Committee for European Nuclear Disarmament (END). He has been a guest speaker to the peace movements in Finland, Denmark, Norway, West Germany, Belgium, France, Ireland, and Iceland. While acting as visiting professors at Brown University, Thompson and his wife Dorothy were welcomed at peace-movement rallies in several parts of the United States.

E. P. Thompson is also the author of *The Making of the English Working Class, Whigs and Hunters,* and *William Morris,* and a co-author of *Albion's Fatal Tree*. He is author of the historic pamphlet and a coeditor of the book *Protest and Survive*.